The LOVE of Money is EVOL

How to Become the Master of Money

Pao Chang

Acknowledgments

I would like to thank God for giving me the wisdom to write this book. Without His help and guidance, I would not have been able to finish this work. I give Him all the glory, honor, and praise. I also would like to thank my wife for supporting and encouraging me to write this book. Thank you, my love, for believing in me.

Table of Contents

Introduction

The most pivotal invention ever conceived by man to facilitate trade and amass wealth is money. Since its inception, money has gone through several transformations, each enhancing its portability and efficiency. Today, billions of people all over the earth use money daily, yet most of them still do not understand where the value of money comes from. Typically, people perceive money as a financial instrument that enables them to trade goods and services without resorting to barter. Because of their perception, they believe that money has value. What they do not realize is that money, in itself, holds no intrinsic value. Those who have endured the ravages of hyperinflation can attest to the potential worthlessness of money. If everyone stops using money today, money becomes worthless. Thus, the value of money does not emanate from the money itself; it is derived from the people. Within every individual—man, woman, and child—is the breath of God that gives them life. It is this very life force that empowers individuals to give things value and transform raw materials into valuable goods.

It is important to understand that money acts as a medium or vessel for storing your labor and the economic energy of nations. When you earn a wage, you are essentially exchanging your time and energy for that wage. Therefore, money represents your expended time and energy. The manner in which you use your time and energy can increase your monetary worth. Consider energy as a form of raw material. Just as raw materials like iron or wood can be transformed into valuable products, enriching the creator through the sale of these products at a price higher than the cost of the raw materials, so too can the raw energy of your mind and body be harnessed to create something beneficial for others. By improving the lives of others with what you create, you increase the value of your time and energy to society.

To understand how you can increase the value of your time and energy, consider this analogy: A barren land in the middle of nowhere has little value. However, if people venture to this land and build beautiful houses and infrastructure, the land's value will rise significantly. Likewise, when you use your time and energy to create something valuable and persuade people to purchase or invest in it, you can substantially increase the value of your time and energy. This enhancement makes it easier for money and wealth to gravitate towards you.

Remember, on a deeper level, money represents your time and energy. Once this truth is truly grasped, it becomes evident that money serves as a financial tool that enhances your ability to utilize time and energy more efficiently. This, in turn, gives you more time to enjoy life and take control of your financial destiny. Such insights form the core purpose of this book. This book is not written to give you financial or legal advice but rather to teach you how to become the master of money. Once you become the master of money, you do not have to worry about being a slave of money because money no longer controls your life. "No man can serve two masters: for either he will hate the one, and love the other; or else he will hold to the one, and despise the other. Ye cannot serve God and mammon" (Matthew 6:24).

Chapter 1
The Spiritual Power of Money and the Origin of Debt

¹⁰ For the love of money is the root of all evil: which while some coveted after, they have erred from the faith, and pierced themselves through with many sorrows. (1 Timothy 6:10)

Is money the root of all evil? To unravel this question, one must delve into the spiritual realm, examining the origins of the word evil and delving into the sacred book that encompasses the history of the heavens and the earth and the revelations of God. In 1 Timothy 6:10, the word evil is a translation of the Greek word κακῶν (*kakós*), meaning "bad, evil."[1] One of the origins of the word evil is the Old English word *yfel* (Kentish *evel*), which means "bad, vicious, ill, wicked." It also encompasses this meaning: "anything that causes injury, anything that harms or is likely to harm; a malady or disease."[2]

The sacred book that encompasses the history of the heavens and the earth and the revelations of God is the Bible, also called the Holy Bible or the Christian Bible. The Bible is the foundation of the Christian faith and has important knowledge that reveals the origin of evil. Within its pages lies valuable knowledge, including Chapter 28 of the Book of Ezekiel, which offers profound insights into the origin of evil. But before delving into that chapter, let us delve deeper into the spiritual significance of the word evil.

The word evil has a strong connection to the word devil. Have you ever noticed that the word **devil** contains the word **evil** within it? This linguistic correlation underscores a deeper spiritual truth. According to *An American Dictionary of the English Language* (1828), the word devil is defined as follows: "In the Christian theology, an evil spirit or being; a fallen angel, expelled from heaven for rebellion against God; the chief of the apostate angels; the implacable enemy and tempter of the human race. In the New Testament, the word is frequently and erroneously used for demon."[3]

It is important to understand that evil is the opposite of live. This notion is evident when examining the spelling of the word live. When the word **live** is spelled backward, it forms the word **evil**. Does this linguistic connection mean that live and evil are opposites? To delve into this question, let us explore some words and their definitions associated with both concepts. As a verb, live encompasses this meaning: "to continue; to be permanent; not to perish" or "to be animated; to have the vital principle; to have the bodily functions in operation, or in a capacity to operate, as respiration, circulation of blood, secretions, etc.; applied to animals."[4] It also means "to have life, as an organism; be alive; be capable of vital functions" or "to continue to have life; remain alive."[5]

The noun for live is living or life, which means "the condition that distinguishes organisms from inorganic objects and dead organisms, being manifested by growth through metabolism, reproduction, and the power of adaptation to environment through changes originating internally."[6] The noun life can also mean "in a general sense, that state of animals and plants, or of an organized being, in which its natural functions and motions are performed, or in which its organs are capable of performing their functions [...]" or "in animals, animation; vitality; and in man, that state of being in which the soul and body are united."[7]

The opposite of life is death. One of the definitions of death is "the act of dying; the end of life; the total and permanent cessation of all the vital functions of an organism."[8] Death can also mean "separation or alienation of the soul from God; a being under the dominion of sin, and destitute of grace or divine life; called spiritual *death*."[9] Death is intrinsically linked with evil, which arises from sin. As an adjective, evil signifies "morally wrong or bad; immoral; wicked."[10] As a noun, it (moral evil) means "[...] any deviation of a moral agent from the rules of conduct prescribed to him by God, or by legitimate human authority; or it is any violation of the plain principles of justice and rectitude."[11] Evil is the result of sin, which leads to spiritual death. Hence, the verse Romans 6:23: "For the wages of sin *is* death; but the gift of God *is* eternal life through Jesus Christ our Lord."

Because death is closely intertwined with evil, and evil is the opposite of live/life, both death and evil are opposed to good. As an adjective, good means "morally excellent; virtuous; righteous; pious."[12] The etymology of good can be traced back to the Old English word *god,* meaning "that which is good, a good thing; goodness; advantage, benefit; gift; virtue; property."[13] Good is a character of God, as reflected in the biblical statement that God is good (Matthew 19:17). This connection is further emphasized in the biblical declaration that "God *is* a Spirit" and the Source of life (John 4:24). "The Spirit of God hath made me, and the breath of the Almighty hath given me life" (Job 33:4). The Bible even says that "the Spirit *is* life because of righteousness" (Romans 8:10).

Life flourishes best where there is light because light is essential for life to exist and thrive. Light is a quality of God, whereas darkness is a quality of Satan. Light brings life to the world, while darkness brings death. Darkness and evil exist in Satan, but they do not exist in God. The Bible even declares that "God is light, and in him is no darkness at all" (1 John 1:5). Unlike God, man harbors darkness due to being fallen creatures controlled by fear. However, the good news is that man can overcome darkness and fear through the love of God. "There is no fear in love; but perfect love casteth out fear: because fear hath torment. He that feareth is not made perfect in love" (1 John 4:18). The power of love is gentle yet capable of empowering someone to overcome anything, even the fear of death. It is the same power that empowers a mother to protect her child, even at the risk of her own life. Because of its profound influence, love is an essential component of God's greatest commandment.

[36] Master, which *is* the great commandment in the law? [37] Jesus said unto him, Thou shalt **love** the Lord

thy God with all thy heart, and with all thy soul, and with all thy mind. [38] This is the first and great commandment. [39] And the second *is* like unto it, Thou shalt **love** thy neighbour as thyself. [40] On these two commandments hang all the law and the prophets. (Matthew 22:36–40)

Love is the very essence of God; therefore, to truly know God, you must love Him with every fiber of your being and love your neighbors as yourself. "He that loveth not knoweth not God; for God is love" (1 John 4:8). Love is God's perfect character, which is why perfect love has the power to cast out fear, rendering evil powerless against the perfect love of God.

You may wonder, what does love have to do with answering the question: is money the root of all evil? Understanding love is the key to finding the answer to this question. Love is the opposite of evil. This is evident when examining the spelling of the word love; when spelled backward, it forms the word "evol," pronounced the same as evil. Thus, phonetically, the words **evol** and **evil** are the same. The reverse spelling of the word love reveals that evol/evil is the opposite of love.

Let us revisit 1 Timothy 6:10. In the first sentence of that verse, it says, "For the **love** of money is the root of all evil." Did you notice the presence of the word love in that sentence? When people love money, they will eventually love money more than God. This "love" for money is not genuine love but rather evol/evil, as it turns money into an idol, which is a false god. Money itself is not evil; it is the **love** of money that is the root of all evil. This love of money motivated Judas Iscariot to betray Jesus for thirty pieces of silver.

Money is neutral in the sense that it has no life and does not have the free will to choose between good and evil. The notion that money is evil does not align with biblical principles. If money were evil, it would create a contradiction within the Bible, which is the infallible Word of God. Since God cannot lie because there is no darkness in Him, the Bible cannot contain contradictions. When people perceive contradictions in the Bible, it is often due to a misunderstanding of the verses or inaccuracies in translation. For instance, Isaiah 45:7 states, "I form the light, and create darkness: I make peace, and create evil: I the LORD do all these *things*." In this verse, the word evil refers to calamity or disaster rather than moral evil, illustrating the importance of understanding the context and nuances of biblical passages.

When most people read Isaiah 45:7, they often interpret it as implying that God created evil or more specifically moral evil. However, moral evil is not a created thing but rather a choice contrary to God's holy laws.[14] To be more specific, moral evil is the result of a choice that does not conform to God's holy laws. For instance, when a man chooses to harm another man and acts on it, he transgresses the holy laws of God and gives rise to evil, allowing evil to corrupt his mind. Therefore, the belief that God created moral evil lacks truth and is not supported by the Scripture. The Bible says that "God is light, and in him is no darkness at all" (1 John 1:5), revealing that God is absolutely good. Because God is absolutely good, He only creates things that are good. The evidence of this can be found in the last verse of Genesis Chapter 1, which was written before the Fall of Man. "And God saw every thing that he had made, and, behold, it was very good. And the evening and the morning were the sixth day" (Genesis 1:31).

Let us turn our attention back to the verse Isaiah 45:7. When analyzing the words in Isaiah 45:7, one notices a juxtaposition of opposites. The first clause of Isaiah 45:7 says, "I form the light, and create darkness." Darkness is simply the absence of light. Therefore, light and darkness are direct opposites. Take note that you can turn on the light to dispel darkness or turn off the light to manifest darkness by flipping a light switch, but you cannot turn on the darkness to dispel light. Moving to the second clause, "I make peace, and create evil," a similar pattern emerges. Here, however, a subtler distinction arises. Peace and evil are not direct opposites as light and darkness are, so something is off here. To grasp the intended meaning, delving into the original Hebrew text is imperative.

In Hebrew, peace translates to שלום (*shalom*), which derives from a root word denoting wholeness or completeness. As for the word evil, the Hebrew word is רע (*ra*). This Hebrew word has several meanings: "bad, evil, distress, misery, injury, calamity."[15] The antonym of peace is not evil but war or calamity. Considering the broader context of Isaiah 45, which revolves around God empowering Cyrus, a pagan king, to wage war on Babylon and deliver His people from Babylonian captivity, the use of the word evil may seem inadequate. This context suggests that the intended meaning may be more aligned with calamity. Hence, the New King James Version (NKJV) revises the second clause of Isaiah 45:7 to read: "I make peace and create calamity." Some people perceive the creation of calamity as an evil act.

7

However, this perspective misunderstands the governance of God. Calamities occur as a result of God's judgment, which is always righteous. Without such judgment upon those who perpetrate evil deeds, God would not be righteous, good, and holy.

One of the most important laws through which God judges people and nations is the Law of Seedtime and Harvest. This spiritual law is mentioned in Genesis 8:22: "While the earth remaineth, seedtime and harvest, and cold and heat, and summer and winter, and day and night shall not cease." It is also mentioned in Galatians 6:7: "Be not deceived; God is not mocked: for whatsoever a man soweth, that shall he also reap."

To understand the Law of Seedtime and Harvest, it is essential to know that thoughts and words are spiritual seeds. However, spoken words act as the vessels that carry these thoughts (spiritual seeds) into the external world. Every time you speak words, you cast your thoughts/seeds into the external world. Therefore, whenever you speak words, you sow (plant) seeds. Once you understand this, it becomes clear that a good harvest is the result of sowing good seeds. Conversely, sowing bad seeds yields a bad harvest, manifesting unpleasant and painful experiences in your life. In simple words, the principle of "what goes around comes around" or "you reap what you sow" summarizes this concept. The Law of Seedtime and Harvest governs everything in the universe. It is one of the reasons that God warned Adam about the consequence of sowing a bad seed in Genesis 2:16-17:

   [16] And the LORD God commanded the man, saying,

Of every tree of the garden thou mayest freely eat: [17]
But of the tree of the knowledge of good and evil,
thou shalt not eat of it: for in the day that thou eatest
thereof thou shalt surely die.

Understanding the Law of Seedtime and Harvest and applying that understanding to your life is one of the keys to manifesting money, wealth, and abundance. In Chapter 3 and 4, we will explore how to manifest money and wealth, as well as how to take control of your finances and make money work for you. This will empower you to become the master of your money. In the meantime, let us delve deeper into the origin of evil and the spiritual power of money. This exploration will help you understand why money is not evil but can be utilized to control your energy (labor), particularly through debt. Furthermore, it will shed light on why money serves as a vessel for storing the economic energy of nations.

One of the keys to understanding the origin of evil is to know that evil is one of the fruits of sin. According to 1 John 3:4, sin is the transgression of the law: "Whosoever committeth sin transgresseth also the law: for sin is the transgression of the law." Therefore, whenever people transgress the law of God, they commit sin and allow evil to enter their hearts. While God did not intend for evil and sin to be part of His creation, the gift of free will inherently carries the potential for rebellion. With free will, intelligent beings can choose to either obey or disobey the laws of God. Keep in mind that the laws of God are perfect and righteous.

Throughout history, intelligent beings with free will had obeyed the laws of God until the rebellion led by Lucifer, an anointed angel of astounding knowledge, beauty, and power.

Lucifer was one of God's most powerful angels because of his profound understanding of the power of words and sound, which are the means through which God speaks the images in His mind into manifestation.

> [13] Thou hast been in Eden the garden of God; every precious stone *was* thy covering, the sardius, topaz, and the diamond, the beryl, the onyx, and the jasper, the sapphire, the emerald, and the carbuncle, and gold: the workmanship of thy tabrets and of thy pipes was prepared in thee in the day that thou wast created. [14] Thou *art* the anointed cherub that covereth; and I have set thee *so*: thou wast upon the holy mountain of God; thou hast walked up and down in the midst of the stones of fire. [15] Thou *wast* perfect in thy ways from the day that thou wast created, till iniquity was found in thee. [16] By the multitude of thy merchandise they have filled the midst of thee with violence, and thou hast sinned: therefore I will cast thee as profane out of the mountain of God: and I will destroy thee, O covering cherub, from the midst of the stones of fire. [17] Thine heart was lifted up because of thy beauty, thou hast corrupted thy wisdom by reason of thy brightness: I will cast thee to the ground, I will lay thee before kings, that they may behold thee. (Ezekiel 28:13–17)

When Lucifer sinned and rebelled against God, man had not yet been created. Therefore, Lucifer is the originator of evil, not man. By sinning, Lucifer transgressed the laws of God and became a vessel for the expression of evil. As a result of his transgression, evil grew like a virus, infecting the minds of many intelligent beings. According to the Book of Revelation, Lucifer successfully persuaded one-third of the angels in heaven to join his war against God. Lucifer was blinded by pride, causing him to believe that he could overthrow God. However, the outcome of this rebellion was defeat for Lucifer and his army, and they were cast out of heaven.

> [7] And there was war in heaven: Michael and his angels fought against the dragon; and the dragon fought and his angels, [8] And prevailed not; neither was their place found any more in heaven. [9] And the great dragon was cast out, that old serpent, called the Devil, and Satan, which deceiveth the whole world: he was cast out into the earth, and his angels were cast out with him. (Revelation 12:7–9)

While on earth, Lucifer, now called Satan, awaited an opportunity to destroy God's most cherished creation: man. When God created man, He created them in His own image and likeness, endowing them with the capacity to love Him and reflect His character. Before the creation of man, no other created being, such as angels, had the capacity to love God in the same manner as He loved His creatures. Because man is created in the image and likeness of God, man is the highest created being, surpassing even the angels in authority. This reality rankled Satan, stoking his jealousy toward man. Thus, he devised a cunning plan to destroy man. He put his plan into action by using the serpent to tempt and deceive Eve to eat the fruit of the tree of knowledge of good and evil.

> [1] Now the serpent was more subtil than any beast of the field which the LORD God had made. And he said unto the woman, Yea, hath God said, Ye shall not eat of every tree of the garden? [2] And the woman said unto the serpent, We may eat of the fruit of the trees of the garden: [3] But of the fruit of the tree which *is* in the midst of the garden, God hath said, Ye shall not eat of it, neither shall ye touch it, lest ye die. [4] And the serpent said unto the woman, Ye shall not surely die: [5] For God doth know that in the day ye eat thereof, then your eyes shall be opened, and ye shall be as gods, knowing good and evil. (Genesis 3:1-5)

Satan is adept at using words to deceive and sow doubt in people's minds. Because of his mastery of words, Satan was able to deceive Eve into believing a lie and redirect her focus towards the one tree that produces the fruits of sin. To grasp one of Satan's motivations for enticing Eve to eat the fruit of the tree of knowledge of good and evil, we need to study Genesis 2:16 and 2:17. "And the LORD God commanded the man, saying, Of **every** tree of the garden thou mayest **freely** eat" (Genesis 2:16). In the verse thereof, the words **every** and **freely** convey abundance, revealing that God created a world full of abundance and devoid of any debt for man. In the next verse, death is forewarned—a consequence of the lack of spiritual food. This lack is caused by sin. "But of **the** tree of the knowledge of good and evil, thou shalt **not** eat of it: for in the day that thou eatest thereof thou shalt surely die" (Genesis 2:17). In this verse, the words **the** and **not** are used to express the one tree that is forbidden to eat; however, in Genesis 2:16, the words **every** and **freely** are used to reveal the multitude of trees available to eat for free. Thus, within these two verses, God offers man with two choices: one leading to abundance and life, and the other leading to deprivation and death.

In Genesis 3:6, Satan successfully tempted Adam and Eve to eat the fruit of the tree of knowledge of good and evil, allowing sin to enter the world. He achieved this by using the persuasive power of words. Words possess the power to program the mind to perceive the world according to their definitions and meanings. In other words, they are the windows through which we see the external world.[16]

Satan, being adept at manipulating words, understands how words can change man's perception of reality, which is why he was able to entice Eve to shift her focus onto what she lacked. This caused her to believe that the thing she lacked was more important than the abundance bestowed upon her by God. Consequently, she succumbed to the temptation and chose to eat the fruit of the tree of knowledge of good and evil. By eating the fruit, she attained knowledge of good and evil but forfeited the vital spiritual food that ensured her immortality.

> [6] And when the woman saw that the tree *was* good for food, and that it *was* pleasant to the eyes, and a tree to be desired to make *one* wise, she took of the fruit thereof, and did eat, and gave also unto her husband with her; and he did eat. [7] And the eyes of them both were opened, and they knew that they *were* naked; and they sewed fig leaves together, and made themselves aprons. (Genesis 3:6–7)

It is important to note that while Eve was deceived by Satan, Adam was not. As stated in 1 Timothy 2:14, "And Adam was not deceived, but the woman being deceived was in the transgression." However, despite being aware that eating the fruit was an act of disobedience against God, Adam failed to protect Eve and chose to eat the fruit when she offered it to him. Consequently, sin entered the world through Adam as well. "Wherefore, as by one man sin entered into the world, and death by sin; and so death passed upon all men, for that all have sinned" (Romans 5:12). By disobeying God's command regarding the tree of the knowledge of good and evil, Adam and Eve committed sin, thereby allowing sin and its fruits to enter the world. Some of the fruits of sin are evil, pride, debt, poverty, pain, suffering, and death.

Before Adam and Eve committed sin, they lived in a world of abundance where everything was freely given to them, devoid of any debt. Their world changed when they rejected life and abundance and chose scarcity and death by eating the forbidden fruit, leading to the inception of debt. This is how debt came into existence in man's kingdom. Among all debts, the worst debt was the debt of sin (Original Sin). "Original Sin is a term that defines the nature of mankind's sinful condition because of Adam's fall. It teaches that all people are corrupted by Adam's sin through natural generation, by which—together with Adam's imputed condemnation—we all enter the world guilty before God."[17] With debt comes scarcity and the need of money to pay for almost everything. Had Adam and Eve not disobeyed God, they would have continued to inhabit a world where everything was freely accessible.

After Adam and Eve fell from grace and were driven out of the Garden of Eden, they had to work hard to reap the fruits of their labor. Essentially, they were tasked with the challenge of cultivating their own food, as they no longer had access to the abundant supply of food in the Garden of Eden. This was a consequence for rejecting life and abundance. Today, man still faces the necessity of hard work to produce the fruits of his labor. However, because of the invention of money and currency, this toil is mitigated for those who possess the wisdom to create wealth.

In the contemporary world, man has developed an economic system where he uses currency to buy goods and services, thereby becoming reliant on it for survival. Because of this, man is willing to exchange his energy (in the form of labor) for currency, so he can use it to buy goods and services to satisfy his hunger for food and material possessions.

The invention of currency was a blessing to man, but it also came with a price, which is the debt of currency. In the wrong hands, this debt can become a tool for widespread enslavement. At its core, currency represents stored energy and embodies the concept of the "flow of energy." This connection is evident when examining the phonetics of the word currency. When spoken aloud, **currency** sounds like the compound noun "current sea." What does a **current** do in a river? It flows or runs to the **sea**. While this may initially seem like a mere coincidence, delving deeper into the origins and meanings of these words reveals an interesting revelation.

The word currency is derived from the Latin word *currens*, the present participle of *currere*, meaning "to run."[18] As for the word current, it is defined by Dictionary.com as "something that flows, as a stream" or "a flowing; flow, as of a river."[19] The dynamic movement of currents is what causes the fresh water of rivers to flow or run to the sea. Upon mingling with sea water, these currents merge, transforming them into the "current sea" or the "current of the sea." Thus, we arrive at the concept of currency as current sea.

An important fact to know about sea water is that it has a high concentration of salt and therefore conducts electricity better than fresh water. Electricity, which is a form of energy, is facilitated by this abundance of electrolytes in sea water. One of the definitions of electrolyte is "any substance that dissociates into ions when dissolved in a suitable medium or melted and thus forms a conductor of electricity."[20] Besides sea water, blood also has electrolytes. In the physical body, electrolytes allow energy, such as electrical impulses, to transmit between cells. Blood, akin to sea water, has currents that carry electrolytes, enabling the transmission of life force—the essence of vitality that animates the physical body. This fact finds resonance in the biblical passage: "For the life of the flesh *is* in the blood: and I have given it to you upon the altar to make an atonement for your souls: for it *is* the blood *that* maketh an atonement for the soul" (Leviticus 17:11).

Upon deeper reflection, the word currency spiritually means the "flow of life force" or "flow of energy." To further substantiate this revelation, let us study the word bank. One of its definitions is "an institution for receiving, lending, exchanging, and safeguarding money and, in some cases, issuing notes and transacting other financial business."[21] Here is one of the legal definitions of bank: "An institution, of great value in the commercial world, empowered to receive deposits of money, to make loans, and to issue its promissory notes, (designed to circulate as money, and commonly called 'bank-notes' or 'bank-bills,') or to perform any one or more of these functions."[22]

An important word to study in the previous definition is money. The word money is defined by *Black's Law Dictionary* (Fourth Edition) using these words: "In its strict technical sense, 'money' means coined metal, usually gold or silver, upon which the government stamp has been impressed to indicate its value. In its more popular sense, 'money' means any currency, tokens, bank-notes, or other circulating medium in general use as the representative of value." Based on this definition, money can also mean currency. However, strictly speaking, there is a difference between money and currency, which we will explore in the next chapter.

Based on the definitions provided earlier, banks are financial institutions that receive deposits of currency (money), make loans, and issue promissory notes. But why do banks receive deposits of currency? On a deeper level, banks receive deposits of currency to control the flow of life force or flow of energy. This connection becomes evident when we study the relation between the words **bank, currency**, and **river**. We have already explored the meanings of bank and currency, so let us study the word river. One of its definitions is "a natural wide flow of fresh water across the land into the sea, a lake, or another river."[23] What is the natural structure of a river that controls the flow of water? The bank! While a bank is primarily known as a financial institution, it also refers to "an undersea elevation rising especially from the continental shelf" or "the rising ground bordering a lake, river, or sea or forming the edge of a cut or hollow."[24] Combining the words **river** and **bank** gives us the word **riverbank**, meaning "the land at either edge of a river."[25] What happens to the currents of a river? They flow to the sea. Hence, the word currency/current-sea.

To connect the dots, corporate banks are like riverbanks because they control the flow of energy, which is represented by the currency/current-sea that people deposit into their bank accounts. This currency serves as a medium or vessel that represents their stored energy. Without this energy to charge currency with power, it has no value and therefore is useless as a medium of exchange. Can you now see the connection between banks, rivers, and currency? Just as riverbanks control the flow of the energy of water, corporate banks control the flow of the energy of people. Corporate banks need to regulate the flow of people's energy to control their currency/current-sea, enabling them to issue debts through loans. Hence, when people default on their debts, loan sharks may come after them to take their currency/current-sea. A shark is a large fish that lives in the sea. If they own commercial corporations and default on their debts, their corporations might be liquidated. The word liquidate means "to settle or pay (a debt)."[26] Did you notice the word **liquid**ate contains the word **liquid** within it? It is about water and energy because water carries the current/currency/current-sea, which is needed to charge debts with value. All debts are "dead" and therefore need to be charged with people's currency (flow of spiritual energy), so the debts can become "alive" and have value.

Because currency is a medium that represents people's

spiritual energy, it can be used by corporations, which are dead bodies, to gain power over them. One of the ways that corporations gain power is by turning currency into debt and using it to control people's spiritual energy. However, when currency is used wisely by individuals, it can eliminate debt and increase prosperity, injecting life into the economy. Most people fail to understand the spiritual power behind money and currency, enabling corporations to enslave them through debt.

It is important to remember that corporations are dead bodies. Devoid of souls and lacking true existence, they cannot confer value upon anything. Only living beings possess the capacity to imbue things, such as currency, with value. This is why corporations, such as banks and governments, need people's currency. Evidence of corporations being lifeless entities can be found in the definition of corporation in *Black's Law Dictionary* (Sixth Edition): "An artificial person or legal entity created by or under the authority of the laws of a state." An artificial person is considered a dead body because it has no life and does not exist in the real world. Another evidence can be found in the abbreviated form of the word **corporations**, which is **corps**. Phonetically, **corps** is the same as **corpse**, which is defined as "a dead body, usually of a human being."[27]

Since all corporations, such as banks and governments, are dead, they like to accumulate debt, which promotes death. Debt is one of the fruits of sin. Debt brings death to the economy; sin brings death to man. Merriam-Webster.com even defines debt as "sin, trespass." Excessive debt inflicts harm on the economy by destroying the purchasing power of its currency, which represents the spiritual energy of the people. Essentially, debt drains the spiritual energy that gives life to the economy. As the economy deteriorates, people have to work harder to make a living, causing hardship and death.

By now, it should be evident that money or currency is not evil; rather, it serves as a medium of exchange to facilitate trade, making it easier for man to exchange his energy (currency) for goods and services. In other words, money makes it easier for you to buy things and provide for your family. According to the Bible, failing to provide for one's household is deemed worse than being an infidel (unbeliever): "But if any provide not for his own, and specially for those of his own house, he hath denied the faith, and is worse than an infidel" (1 Timothy 5:8). Even though money is not evil, the **love** of money can cause people to do evil things. When people love money, they will eventually love it more than God, transforming money into an idol, which is a false god. This transformation allows money to become their master. "No man can serve two masters: for either he will hate the one, and love the other; or else he will hold to the one, and despise the other. Ye cannot serve God and mammon" (Matthew 6:24).

Chapter 2
The Secrets of Fractional Reserve Banking and Fiat Currency

Currency is the most convenient tool for assisting individuals to exchange their time and energy for the fruits of other people's labor. Additionally, currency is the most liquid asset in the world because it is recognized and accepted as a medium of exchange, allowing people to trade goods and services without the need to barter. In a barter system, if a buyer wants to buy a shirt but has only a chicken for exchange, the seller may or may not accept the chicken. Therefore, successful bartering necessitates a double coincidence of wants, meaning that both parties possess goods they are willing to exchange. This made bartering inefficient and inconvenient. With the invention of money and currency, the problem concerning double coincidence of wants was no longer a problem.

In communication, money and currency are often used interchangeably. However, there is a difference between them. Money and currency are similar because they can serve as a medium of exchange and are interchangeable where each unit is the same as the next. In addition, they are a unit of account, portable, durable, and divisible, meaning that they can be exchanged for smaller denominations. But unlike currency, money is a store of value over a long period of time.[1] Money, such as gold and silver, is better at storing value than currency because it is limited in supply and cannot be duplicated easily. Gold and silver are the safest forms of money because they have maintained their value for thousands of years. This is why during an economic crisis, banks always hoard them, especially gold. Strictly speaking, any money that can be duplicated easily is not really money because it does a poor job of storing value. The more a money is duplicated, the more its purchasing power decreases, causing inflation and economic crises.

An important word we need to know its deeper meaning is inflation. One of the definitions of inflation is "a general increase in prices coinciding with a fall in the real value of money."[2] Another of its definition is "a persistent, substantial rise in the general level of prices related to an increase in the volume of money and resulting in the loss of value of currency."[3] Put simply, as more currency is injected into the economy, its worth diminishes, resulting in the loss of value, which in turn causes prices to increase. In simple words, "inflation is an expansion of the currency supply" and "rising prices are merely the symptom."[4] Upon closer examination, inflation is a hidden tax on the people. It is inexpensive for central banks to inject currency into the economy; however, the consequences are far costlier for individuals. Inflation erodes their savings, resulting in a significant loss of currency and wealth. This is how central banks steal people's currency and wealth without their knowledge.

The fact that currency can be used as a hidden tax makes it a very powerful weapon of central banks. On the other hand, it is much harder for central banks to use money as a hidden tax. The attributes of money make money effective for restraining banks, so they do not spend recklessly. Because of this, the banks of today prefer to use currency, enabling them to spend more than they earn. This preferred form of currency is known as fiat currency or fiat money. Here is one of its definitions: "fiat money, in a broad sense, all kinds of money that are made legal tender by a government decree or fiat. The term is, however, usually reserved for legal-tender paper money or coins that have face values far exceeding their commodity values and are not redeemable in gold or silver."[5] The term fiat means "an authoritative decree, sanction, or order."[6] Therefore, fiat money (fiat currency) is "a currency that is decreed and backed by the government that issues it."[7] Fiat currency lacks intrinsic value and is backed by the credit of the government. Consequently, the value of fiat currency is strongly dependent on confidence. Any fiat currency that loses the trust of the people will eventually collapse. In a sense, fiat currency is monopoly money (fake money). Reflecting on this, one might see that the world is becoming more artificial.

Similar to the banks of today, governments also like to spend more than they earn. This is known as deficit spending. In the United States of America, when the government faces a shortfall in funds to cover its expenses, it issues bonds and sells them for currency. This process of issuing bonds is done through the Department of the Treasury. A bond is defined by *Black's Law Dictionary* (Fourth Edition) using these words: "A certificate or evidence of a debt" or "a deed whereby the obligor obliges himself, his heirs, executors and administrators, to pay a certain sum of money to another at a day appointed." Dictionary.com defines it as "a certificate of ownership of a specified portion of a debt due to be paid by a government or corporation to an individual holder and usually bearing a fixed rate of interest."[8] Based on these definitions, a bond is a debt instrument. In other words, "a bond is nothing but a glorified IOU."[9] It is the government's way of saying to investors, "loan me some currency today and I promise I will pay you back the principal plus interest on the due date."[10]

It is important to know that the bonds issued by the U.S. Department of the Treasury become part of the national debt of the United States of America once they are sold to investors through auctions. Many of these investors are high-level bankers. The sale of these bonds effectively turns the U.S. Government into a debtor. The main source of revenue for the U.S. Government is taxation. This means that U.S. citizens are the ones paying for the national debt. Essentially, the currency (flow of energy) of U.S. citizens is utilized by the U.S. Government to pay its debt, so it can avoid bankruptcy. Note that this practice of using citizens to pay the debt of a government is not limited to the United States of America. All countries with central banks are involved in the practice of using citizens to pay for their national debts. This practice is worldwide because the world currently operates under a debt-based financial system known as fractional reserve banking.

After bankers purchase bonds from the U.S. Department of the Treasury, they sell some of those bonds to the Federal Reserve (Fed) through a process known as open market operations. "The Fed conducts open market operations to regulate the supply of money that is on reserve in U.S. banks. The Fed purchases Treasury securities to increase the money supply and sells them to reduce it."[11] One of the problems with this process is that the Fed, which is a private corporation with stockholders, purchases the bonds using a checking account that basically has no bank deposits. Essentially, the Fed is creating "money" out of thin air to purchase these bonds. The Fed uses its bogus checking account to write checks to acquire bonds from bankers, who then exchange the checks for currency. These same bankers then use this currency to purchase more bonds from the U.S. Department of the Treasury.

Every time the U.S. Department of the Treasury sells bonds to investors, and every time the Fed buys bonds from bankers, more debt is injected into the economy, thereby increasing the U.S. national debt. The increase of the national debt means more taxes for citizens to pay, generating more currency for lenders, primarily banks. This is how the Fed and its bankers surreptitiously steal the wealth of U.S. citizens through debt-based financial systems (e.g., fractional reserve banking) and bonds. Remember, a bond is "a certificate or evidence of a debt." Consider this definition of debt: "That which is due from one person to another, whether money, goods, or services; that which one person is bound to pay or perform to another; as the debts of a bankrupt; the debts of a nobleman. It is a common misfortune or vice to be in *debt.*"[12]

When a man is in debt, he gives to another power over his liberty.[13] Evidence of this can be found in the word bondage. The root word of bondage is bond. We already know what the word bond means, so let us study the word bondage. Here is one of the definitions of bondage: "slavery or involuntary servitude; serfdom."[14] Bondage also means "the state of being bound by or subjected to some external power or control."[15]

The agency responsible for making sure U.S. citizens are in bondage to the national debt is the Internal Revenue Service (IRS). According to IRS.gov, the "IRS is a bureau of the Department of the Treasury."[16] Here are some important facts about the Internal Revenue Service: "The IRS has repeatedly argued that, even though Congress did not create the IRS through an act, it is a government agency. It cites the 1971 Supreme Court case *Donaldson v. the United States*, in which the court ruled the IRS is allowed to administer internal revenue laws as an agency would. Also, the IRS points out that the U.S. Code grants the Secretary of the Treasury full authority to enforce tax law and to appoint an agency to do so."[17] The following is a quote from the 1971 Supreme Court case:

> We bear in mind that the Internal Revenue Service is organized to carry out the broad responsibilities of the Secretary of the Treasury under § 7801(a) of the 1954 Code for the administration and enforcement of the internal revenue laws.[18]

Be aware that the IRS is not owned by the Department of the

Treasury but works for it. Most U.S. citizens know that the IRS collects taxes for the federal government, but what they do not realize is that the IRS also functions as a debt collector, which is why it collects debts (Federal Reserve notes) from U.S. citizens to settle the debts of the federal government. To be more specific, the IRS collects income taxes from U.S. citizens, enabling it to transfer the currency collected from the taxes to the Department of the Treasury. This currency is then utilized to pay both the principal and interest on bonds purchased by the Federal Reserve (Fed). The currency collected from income taxes is not used to pay for roads, schools, and public services but to pay interest on bonds held by the bankers who control the fractional reserve banking system. These bankers have a vested interest in accumulating debt because of the interest it generates. More debt means more interest they can collect through tax agencies, such as the IRS.

Most, if not all, financial systems of countries around the world operate within the domain of the fractional reserve banking system. Because of this, the bankers who control this banking system can use it to hoard most of the world's wealth. These bankers like to exploit the international banking system to siphon wealth away from the people of the world, ultimately destroying their standard of living. To understand how the bankers are able to steal people's wealth without their knowledge, it is essential to study the term fractional reserve banking.

> Fractional reserve banking is a system in which only a fraction of bank deposits are required to be available for withdrawal. Banks only need to keep a

27

specific amount of cash on hand and can create loans from the money you deposit. Fractional reserves work to expand the economy by freeing capital for lending. Today, most economies' financial systems use fractional reserve banking.[19]

It is important to know that fractional reserve banking empowers banks to create loans using the currency that customers deposit in their banking accounts. This type of banking allows banks to reserve only a fraction of customers' deposits, hence the term "fractional reserve banking." The fractional reserve ratios can vary, ranging from 10 percent to as low as 1 percent or less. A bank operating with a 10 percent fractional reserve ratio is allowed to reserve 10 percent of customers' deposits and loan 90 percent of the remaining deposits. For example, if a customer deposits 100 dollars, the bank can legally loan 90 dollars of that amount without notifying the customer, leaving only 10 dollars in the customer's account. To create the illusion that the account still has 100 dollars, the bank substitutes the 90 dollars with a bank credit equivalent to 90 dollars. This bank credit is basically an IOU that only exists in a computer register. By crediting the account with a bank credit of 90 dollars, the total currency in the system increases to 190 dollars: 100 dollars from the customer and 90 dollars in the form of a bank credit from the bank. This is how banks create currency out of thin air to expand the currency supply.

The information in the previous paragraph illustrates how a customer's deposit of 100 dollars can be used by a bank with a 10 percent fractional reserve ratio to create 90 dollars' worth of credit. This process allows the bank to lend out 90 percent of the customer's 100 dollars. Now, let us pretend that the customer's deposit is 10,000 dollars and his bank is called Bank X. By using the 10 percent fractional reserve ratio, bank X can issue a bank credit equivalent to 9,000 dollars to replace the customer's 9,000 dollars, thereby allowing it to lend 9,000 dollars to a borrower without impacting the customer's account balance. This creates the illusion that there are still 10,000 dollars in the customer's account, when in reality, only 1,000 dollars remain. This reality can be seen during a bank run, which the bank runs out of cash because it only reserves a fraction of its customers' deposits. Since Bank X can legally loan most of the customer's deposit, it will not hesitate to transfer 90 percent of that deposit to a qualified borrower in the form of a check.

Let us imagine that a borrower wants to borrow 9,000 dollars from Bank X to buy a used car from a seller. Upon approval, Bank X issues a check to the borrower, who then hands it to the seller in exchange for the car. The seller then deposits the check into his account at Bank Y. Following the same fractional reserve ratio, Bank Y can also loan out 90 percent of that deposit. This cycle repeats and repeats, creating more money out of thin air and reducing the purchasing power of the currency.

Under the fractional reserve banking system, an initial deposit of 10,000 dollars in a bank with a 10 percent fractional reserve ratio can be used to create up to 100,000 dollars' worth of currency. This process grants banks access to more credit, but it also injects more currency into the economy, resulting in the rise of prices, commonly known as inflation. This type of currency is destructive to the economy because it is based on debt. All debts are parasitic, meaning that they behave like parasites. Consequently, as the level of debt increases, more life force is needed to support the economy, so it does not collapse and die. This means that people will have to work harder, so they can create more currency (flow of life force) to sustain the economy. Otherwise, the parasitic debt will suck the life energy of the economy until there is nothing left, causing it to collapse and die. In this paragraph, a word that you need to know its deeper meaning is economy. Let us delve into the word economy by first studying its etymology:

> 1530s, "household management," from Latin *oeconomia* (source of French *économie*, Spanish *economia*, German *Ökonomie*, etc.), from Greek *oikonomia* "household management, thrift," from *oikonomos* "manager, steward," from *oikos* "house, abode, dwelling" (cognate with Latin *vicus* "district," *vicinus* "near;" Old English *wic* "dwelling, village," from PIE root *weik- (1) "clan") + *nomos* "managing," from *nemein* "manage" (from PIE root *nem- "assign, allot; take").[20]

One of the modern definitions of economy is "the complex of activities related to the consumption, production, and trade of goods and services, as an ongoing functioning system."[21] *An American Dictionary of the English Language* (1828) defines it using these words: "Primarily, the management, regulation and government of a family or the concerns of a household." Here is another definition of economy from the same dictionary:

A frugal and judicious use of money; that management which expends money to advantage, and incurs no waste; frugality in the necessary expenditure of money. It differs from parsimony, which implies an improper saving of expense. *Economy* includes also a prudent management of all the means by which property is saved or accumulated; a judicious application of time, of labor, and of the instruments of labor.[22]

By studying some of the definitions of economy, it reveals that the word economy has a close association with household management and the **prudent** management of property, time, labor, and money (currency). The word prudent means "wise or judicious in practical affairs; discreet or circumspect; sagacious; sober" or "careful in providing for the future; provident."[23] Therefore, the word economy is intricately tied to the wise management of the property, time, labor, and money (currency) of a household or nation.

The health of the economy is dependent on the flow of currency in the economy. When a nation manages its currency wisely, the economy thrives and the people's standard of living increases. The economy relies on currency to survive because it represents the life energy of the people. Remember, currency spiritually means "flow of life force" or "flow of energy." On a deeper level, the economy operates as an energy system that relies on the life energy of the people to function properly.

Energy is recognized as the key to all activity on earth. Natural science is the study of the sources and control of natural energy, and social science, theoretically expressed as economics, is the study of the sources and control of social energy. Both are bookkeeping systems: mathematics. Therefore, mathematics is the primary energy science. And the bookkeeper can be king if the public can be kept ignorant of the methodology of the bookkeeping.

[...] In the study of energy systems, there always appears three elementary concepts. These are potential energy, kinetic energy, and energy dissipation. And corresponding to these concepts, there are three idealized, essentially pure physical counterparts called passive components.

1. In the science of physical mechanics, the phenomenon of potential energy is associated with a physical property called elasticity or stiffness, and can be represented by a stretched spring. In electronic science, potential energy is stored in a capacitor instead of a spring. This property is called capacitance instead of elasticity or stiffness.

2. In the science of physical mechanics, the phenomenon of kinetic energy is associated with a physical property called inertia or mass, and can be represented by a mass or a flywheel in motion. In electronic science, kinetic energy is stored in an inductor (in a magnetic field) instead of a mass. This

property is called inductance instead of inertia.

3. In the science of physical mechanics, the phenomenon of energy dissipation is associated with a physical property called friction or resistance, and can be represented by a dashpot or other device which converts energy into heat. In electronic science, dissipation of energy is performed by an element called either a resistor or a conductor, the term "resistor" being the one generally used to describe a more ideal device (e.g., wire) employed to convey electronic energy efficiently from one location to another. The property of a resistance or conductor is measured as either resistance or conductance reciprocals.

In economics these three energy concepts are associated with:

1. Economic Capacitance - Capital (money, stock/inventory, investments in buildings and durables, etc.)

2. Economic Conductance - Goods (production flow coefficients)

3. Economic Inductance - Services (the influence of the population of industry on output)

All of the mathematical theory developed in the study of one energy system (e.g., mechanics, electronics, etc.) can be immediately applied in the study of any other energy system (e.g., economics).[24]

Throughout history, specific banking dynasties, such as the Rothschilds, have recognized the connection between the economy and energy. Their understanding of economics in relation to energy is one of the reasons that they have become so rich and powerful, allowing them to control nations and orchestrate wars.

What Mr. Rothschild had discovered was the basic principle of power, influence, and control over people as applied to economics. That principle is "when you assume the appearance of power, people soon give it to you."

Mr. Rothschild had discovered that currency or deposit loan accounts had the required appearance of power that could be used to induce people (inductance, with people corresponding to a magnetic field) into surrendering their real wealth in exchange for a promise of greater wealth (instead of real compensation). They would put up real collateral in exchange for a loan of promissory notes. Mr. Rothschild found that he could issue more notes than he had backing for, so long as he had someone's stock of gold as a persuader to show his customers.

Mr. Rothschild loaned his promissory notes to individuals and to governments. These would create overconfidence. Then he would make money scarce, tighten control of the system, and collect the collateral through the obligation of contracts. The cycle was then repeated. These pressures could be used to ignite a war. Then he would control the availability of currency to determine who would win the war. That government which agreed to give him control of its economic system got his support.

[...] In this structure, credit, presented as a pure element called "currency," has the appearance of capital, but is in effect negative capital. Hence, it has the appearance of service, but is in fact, indebtedness or debt. It is therefore an economic inductance instead of an economic capacitance, and if balanced in no other way, will be balanced by the negation of population (war, genocide). The total goods and services represent real capital called the gross national product, and currency may be printed up to this level and still represent economic capacitance; but currency printed beyond this level is subtractive, represents the introduction of economic inductance, and constitutes notes of indebtedness.

War is therefore the balancing of the system by killing the true creditors (the public which we have taught to exchange true value for inflated currency) and falling back on whatever is left of the resources of nature and regeneration of those resources.[25]

The true creditors have always been the people because they have spirits and therefore are living beings. In contrast, banks and governments are imaginary bodies that have no spirits. All spirits come from God, the Source of life and value. Only living beings can rightfully be deemed creditors because their life energy is what gives value to currency.

The bankers who control the fractional reserve banking system like wars because wars make them enormous amounts of currency through the issuance of financial instruments (e.g., promissory notes) to finance the warring nations. Furthermore, wars allow these bankers to kill the true creditors (the people) without direct involvement. By killing the true creditors, the bankers can erase the debts owed to the creditors, thereby enabling them to make even more currency. The currency that gives bankers the means to create almost unlimited financial instruments for lending to individuals and governments is called fiat currency, also known as fiat money.

> Fiat money, in a broad sense, all kinds of money that are made legal tender by a government decree or fiat. The term is, however, usually reserved for legal-tender paper money or coins that have face values far exceeding their commodity values and are not redeemable in gold or silver."[26]

Remember, fiat currency lacks intrinsic value and is backed by the credit of the government. This means that the value of fiat currency is strongly dependent on confidence. Because fiat currency is backed by credit, it can be easily created out of thin air. However, any currency created in this manner lacks value. Therefore, when such currency is injected into the banking system, it sucks up the value of the currency already in circulation. This decreases the purchasing power of the currency and causes inflation, which in turn increases the prices of goods and services. As the cost of living rises, people may need to work multiple jobs to pay their expenses and bills. Inflation causes people to spend less and reduce their investments in the stock market, leading to economic recessions.

One of the flaws of the fractional reserve banking system is its dependence on debt for functionality. Therefore, without debt, it cannot operate effectively. However, the problem with debt is that there is a limit to how much it can grow. Over time, debt can swell to a magnitude where it becomes unsustainable, ultimately leading to the destruction of the economy. Until the people of the world stop supporting the fractional reserve banking system and transition to a monetary system not based on debt, they risk becoming slaves of debt and losing all their property to the bankers.

Once you comprehend the information in this chapter, it becomes evident that the fractional reserve banking system, along with its fiat currency, is currently the biggest Ponzi scheme ever created by the bankers. This banking system is parasitic because it siphons currency from hardworking citizens to the scammers, which are the bankers who control the fractional reserve banking system. It also sucks currency from future generations, so its owners (the bankers) can spend it today. This means that the children who are not even born yet may inherit a world burdened by insurmountable debt. The bankers and their fractional reserve banking system play a very big role in enslaving future generations with debt. Additionally, individuals burdened by excessive debt exacerbate the issue by perpetuating the cycle. "No generation has a right to contract debts greater than can be paid off during the course of its own existence."[27]

The bankers and their fractional reserve banking system may seem invincible, but what they do not want you to realize is that their banking system is fragile and has no power without the support of the people. They rely on people's ignorance to keep their banking system running smoothly. These bankers are skillful at deceiving people because they are, in a sense, magicians. With a stroke of the pen, they manifest money out of thin air, wielding it to control the world.

When enough people become aware of how the banking system works and wake up to the truth that they have the power to change the world, the bankers and their fractional reserve banking system will lose power over them. The power has always resided in the people because inside each of them is the source of life that gives value to everything, such as currency. This is why currency spiritually means "flow of life force" or "flow of energy."

It is important to remember that currency or money itself is not evil. It is what people do with it that makes it a tool for good or evil. The practices of the bankers of the fractional reserve banking system are deemed evil because they exploit currency to keep people in bondage to debt, depriving them of their wealth and property. These bankers worship Satan and love money more than God, which is why they want to rule the world through their satanic banking system. The fractional reserve banking system was created by the bankers to steal wealth from the children of God, so they can use it to help their satanic master build his kingdom of darkness on earth. To prevent this, we need to create a better monetary system, so we can stop using their satanic banking system to do business.

Man is now at a crossroad where he needs to choose between two new monetary systems: God's monetary system or Satan's monetary system. God's monetary system is backed by gold and is fair and open. On the other hand, Satan's monetary system is a debt-based monetary system with the goal of being entirely digital, so it can be used to implement the mark of the beast. The digital currency that Satan wants to use to rule the world is called central bank digital currency (CBDC). God's monetary system will also utilize digital technology but is backed by gold and not based on debt. The choices people make this year (2024) and next year (2025) will play a significant role in determining which monetary system will be used to run the economy of the world. Choose wisely so that you and your children may live in prosperity.

> [19] I call heaven and earth to record this day against you, *that* I have set before you life and death, blessing and cursing: therefore choose life, that both thou and thy seed may live: (Deuteronomy 30:19)

Chapter 3
How to Become
the Master of Money

⁴ Unto you, O men, I call; and my voice *is* to the sons of man. ⁵ O ye simple, understand wisdom: and, ye fools, be ye of an understanding heart. ⁶ Hear; for I will speak of excellent things; and the opening of my lips *shall be* right things. ⁷ For my mouth shall speak truth; and wickedness *is* an abomination to my lips. ⁸ All the words of my mouth *are* in righteousness; *there is* nothing froward or perverse in them. ⁹ They *are* all plain to him that understandeth, and right to them that find knowledge. ¹⁰ Receive my instruction, and not silver; and knowledge rather than choice gold. ¹¹ For wisdom *is* better than rubies; and all the things that may be desired are not to be compared to it. (Proverbs 8:4-11).

Wisdom is the key to mastery. Therefore, to be the master of money requires wisdom. A rich man who lacks wisdom is poorer than a wise man who lacks money. This is because wisdom protects and multiplies wealth. A wise man knows that wisdom can buy money, but money cannot buy wisdom. One of the reasons that wisdom can buy money is because wisdom improves a man's skill set, leading to mastery. Mastering his skill set increases his value and gives him leverage in negotiation, allowing him to make more money than the average man. To understand why being the master of money requires wisdom, you need to know what wisdom is on a deeper level. Let us explore what wisdom is by first reading one of its definitions:

> The right use or exercise of knowledge; the choice of laudable ends, and of the best means to accomplish them. This is *wisdom* in act, effect, or practice. If *wisdom* is to be considered as a faculty of the mind, it is the faculty of discerning or judging what is most just, proper and useful, and if it is to be considered as an acquirement, it is the knowledge and use of what is best, most just, most proper, most conducive to prosperity or happiness. *Wisdom* in the first sense, or practical *wisdom* is nearly synonymous with discretion. It differs somewhat from prudence, in this respect; prudence is the exercise of sound judgment in avoiding evils; *wisdom* is the exercise of sound judgment either in avoiding evils or attempting good. Prudence then is a species, of which *wisdom* is the genus.[1]

Based on the above definition, wisdom is the exercise of

knowledge in a just, proper, and efficient way. In the previous sentence, a word you should pay attention to is knowledge. To acquire wisdom, you first need to have knowledge so you can learn how to exercise that knowledge properly. What is knowledge? Before we answer that question, let us read one of the definitions of knowledge: "A clear and certain perception of that which exists, or of truth and fact; the perception of the connection and agreement, or disagreement and repugnancy of our ideas."[2] Knowledge also means "acquaintance with facts, truths, or principles, as from study or investigation; general erudition."[3] Once you have knowledge, you need an understanding of it, so you can apply it in your life properly, leading to wisdom. The word understanding means "comprehending; apprehending the ideas or sense of another, or of a writing; learning or being informed."[4] Here is another definition of understanding:

> The faculty of the human mind by which it apprehends the real state of things presented to it, or by which it receives or comprehends the ideas which others express and intend to communicate. The *understanding* is called also the intellectual faculty. It is the faculty by means of which we obtain a great part of our knowledge.[5]

In summary, knowledge is the accumulation of truth, understanding is the assimilation of truth, and wisdom is the application of truth.[6] In other words, the first step to wisdom is accumulating truth (knowledge). The second step is assimilating truth (understanding). The word assimilate means "to take into the mind and thoroughly understand."[7]

The third and last step is applying truth in a good and proper way, which leads to wisdom. This last step is usually the hardest and takes more time than the other two steps, which is why wisdom comes with age. As people age, their physical strength diminishes, but if they have wisdom, that wisdom will strengthen their minds and spirits. "Wisdom strengtheneth the wise more than ten mighty *men* which are in the city" (Ecclesiastes 7:19).

Knowledge is something that everyone has, but without understanding, that knowledge has little power to transform the mind. Most people have an understanding of various degrees; however, only a small percentage of them have enough wisdom. This is why many people do not know how to improve their lives spiritually, mentally, and financially. If you want to do very well in life and be rich in these areas, you need to acquire great knowledge first. To do this, you must fear God. "The fear of the Lord *is* the beginning of knowledge: *but* fools despise wisdom and instruction" (Proverbs 1:7).

> [3] Through wisdom is an house builded; and by understanding it is established: [4] And by knowledge shall the chambers be filled with all precious and pleasant riches. [5] A wise man *is* strong; yea, a man of knowledge increaseth strength. (Proverbs 24:3–5)

It is important to understand that fearing the Lord is not the same as fearing a monster. A wise man fears the Lord like how a child fears his father. A loving father will chasten his child to discipline him so he knows the difference between right and wrong; that way, he does not grow up to become an evil man. Through the process of chastening, the child learns to fear, respect, and honor his father. Any father who does not discipline his child does not love him enough. A wise man also fears the LORD because he knows the LORD is absolutely good and righteous. Furthermore, the LORD is the Judge over all the earth and has the authority and power to command souls to eternal punishment in hell for transgressing His holy laws. To transgress these holy laws is to commit sin. "Whosoever committeth sin transgresseth also the law: for sin is the transgression of the law" (1 John 3:4).

A man who commits sin against God is like a soldier who commits treason against a king. The penalty for that kind of treason is death. Committing sin is that serious, which is why the only punishment that completely satisfies the penalty of sin is death. Therefore, if the LORD does not command sinners to eternal death for transgressing His holy laws, He would not be absolutely good and righteous. This is why the LORD disciplines us to fear, respect, and honor Him, so that we may stay away from evil and obey His holy laws, preventing us from being judged and cast into hell. The LORD does not want anyone to perish in hell because it is a place worse than death: a place where the soul is scorched by unquenchable fire and tormented for eternity. "And they shall go forth, and look upon the carcases of the men that have transgressed against me: for their worm shall not die, neither shall their fire be quenched; and they shall be an abhorring unto all flesh" (Isaiah 66:24). Once you realize that the LORD is absolutely good and righteous, you will know that the fear of the LORD is a blessing because it helps you make better decisions, preventing you from living a sinful life.

Let us turn our attention back to knowledge. When you fear God, He is willing to teach you His knowledge, which is not the same as man's knowledge. God's knowledge contains revelations, which are designed to help you unveil the mystery of His creation, allowing you to see and understand Truth. Understanding the knowledge of God is very powerful, as it can be used to gain great wisdom and power. A man who fears God will avoid using divine knowledge for selfish reasons, such as gaining power over others. Because of this, God is willing to teach you more of His knowledge when you fear Him. Never forget that God is the Source of true knowledge, understanding, and wisdom, and He will restrict your access to His knowledge unless you fear Him. With great knowledge comes great responsibility.

> In order to develop the fear of the Lord, we must recognize God for who He is. We must glimpse with our spirits the power, might, beauty, and brilliance of the Lord God Almighty (Revelation 11:17; Hosea 12:5; Isaiah 6:1-5). Those who fear the Lord have a continual awareness of Him, a deep reverence for Him, and sincere commitment to obey Him.[8]

It is important to know that knowledge without wisdom has little usefulness. A man who graduated with a master's degree in finance has a lot of financial knowledge, but if he lacks the wisdom to apply that knowledge in his life, he will not be able to achieve financial freedom. Take note that knowledge without wisdom can lead to pride. The problem with pride is that it causes people to be arrogant and spiritually blind, preventing them from seeing the truth. Therefore, pride always corrupts the mind and motivates people to live a sinful life, causing them to rebel against God. "The wicked, through the pride of his countenance, will not seek *after God*: God *is* not in all his thoughts" (Psalms 10:4). Pride leads to sin because pride is not of God. "For all that *is* in the world, the lust of the flesh, and the lust of the eyes, and the pride of life, is not of the Father, but is of the world" (1 John 2:16). Pride also leads people to self-worship and destruction. "Pride goeth before destruction, and an haughty spirit before a fall" (Proverbs 16:18). Lucifer, an anointed angel of astounding beauty, knowledge, and wisdom, was cast out of heaven because of pride. Lucifer's pride led him to convince one-third of the angels in heaven to rebel against God, causing destruction throughout heaven.

Because knowledge without wisdom leads to destruction, it is important to seek knowledge and then contemplate that knowledge with God, so you can apply it to gain wisdom. With wisdom comes wealth and riches. King Solomon became the richest man in the world because he sought wisdom earnestly. Solomon was the son of King David. Shortly after David died, God appeared to Solomon in a dream and told him to ask what He should give him. Solomon replied to the Lord by asking Him to give him wisdom and knowledge, so he could judge the people righteously.

> [11] And God said to Solomon, Because this was in thine heart, and thou hast not asked riches, wealth, or honour, nor the life of thine enemies, neither yet hast asked long life; but hast asked wisdom and knowledge for thyself, that thou mayest judge my

people, over whom I have made thee king: [12] Wisdom and knowledge *is* granted unto thee; and I will give thee riches, and wealth, and honour, such as none of the kings have had that *have been* before thee, neither shall there any after thee have the like. (2 Chronicles 1:11-12)

Note that King Solomon only asked for wisdom and knowledge, yet God gave him wisdom and knowledge along with riches, wealth, and honor. Why did God give Solomon these treasures, even though he did not ask for them? One of the reasons is that wisdom comes with riches, wealth, and honor. In other words, they are some of the fruits of wisdom. Solomon knew how precious wisdom was and that God was the Source of true wisdom. Therefore, he relied on God for knowledge and understanding. The wisdom that God put in Solomon's heart made him so rich that his kingdom was filled with gold; even his drinking vessels were made of gold. If Solomon were alive today, his wealth would be worth trillions of dollars. Note that I am referring to real wealth, not the fake wealth of today that is backed by credits and IOUs.

[21] And all king Solomon's drinking vessels *were of* gold, and all the vessels of the house of the forest of Lebanon *were of* pure gold; none *were of* silver: it was nothing accounted of in the days of Solomon. [22] For the king had at sea a navy of Tharshish with the navy of Hiram: once in three years came the navy of Tharshish, bringing gold, and silver, ivory, and apes, and peacocks. [23] So king Solomon exceeded all the kings of the earth for riches and for wisdom. [24] And

all the earth sought to Solomon, to hear his wisdom, which God had put in his heart. [25] And they brought every man his present, vessels of silver, and vessels of gold, and garments, and armour, and spices, horses, and mules, a rate year by year. (1 Kings 10:21-25)

People came to see King Solomon to hear his wisdom, and they also brought him gifts. They were more interested in his wisdom than his riches. Also, note that Solomon's wisdom was not always free because he charged them a rate year by year. Because of Solomon's wisdom, many kings and queens came to him for knowledge, and they paid him enormous amounts of money to consult and mentor them so they could acquire his wisdom. One of them was the Queen of Sheba. According to Chapter 10 of 1 Kings, she gave King Solomon 120 talents of gold, plus spices and precious stones, to hear and see his wisdom.

In ancient times, the weight of a talent of gold varied from country to country. In general, a talent of gold weighs anywhere between 56 to 125 pounds or more. Let us assume that a talent of gold weighs about 90 pounds, which is equivalent to 40.8 kilograms. Note that the gold of today is measured in ounces, not talents. Keep in mind that 1 pound equals 16 ounces. As of November 2023, an ounce of gold is worth about 2,000 dollars. Therefore, after doing the math, the price of 120 talents of gold is 345,600,000 dollars. If we were to include the price of the spices and precious stones in the math, the amount of money that the Queen of Sheba paid King Solomon would be roughly half a billion dollars. Why did she pay Solomon so much money just to hear and see his wisdom? One reason is that with great wisdom comes great wealth, prosperity, and authority. The wisdom she acquired from Solomon made her realize that her kingdom would be blessed with riches, wealth, and honor, as long as she obeyed the wisdom of God.

Solomon had great knowledge, but unlike most people, he also had great understanding, giving him the insight to apply his knowledge to increase his wisdom. Solomon's wisdom helped him build great businesses, which were some of the main keys to his success. Without building great businesses, it would have been impossible for Solomon to become the richest man on earth. According to 1 Kings 10:14, Solomon's businesses made six hundred and sixty-six talents of gold yearly or about 2 billion dollars every year, not including other goods (e.g., silver, precious stones, etc.). Solomon was able to surpass all the kings of the earth in riches and wisdom because he built a kingdom and several businesses on the foundation of the wisdom of God. This wisdom comes with prudence, riches, honor, understanding, and righteousness; furthermore, it gives kings the authority to rule and decree. Therefore, those who love and obey the wisdom of God and use it wisely will not lack prudence, riches, honor, understanding, righteousness, and authority.

[12] **I wisdom dwell with prudence**, and find out knowledge of witty inventions. [13] The fear of the LORD *is* to hate evil: pride, and arrogancy, and the evil way, and the froward mouth, do I hate. [14] Counsel *is* mine, and sound wisdom: **I *am* understanding**; I have strength. [15] **By me kings reign, and princes decree justice**. [16] By me princes rule, and

nobles, *even* all the judges of the earth. [17] I love them that love me; and those that seek me early shall find me. [18] **Riches and honour *are* with me**; *yea*, durable riches and **righteousness.** [19] **My fruit *is* better than gold**, yea, than fine gold; and my revenue than choice silver. [20] I lead in the way of righteousness, in the midst of the paths of judgment: [21] That I may cause **those that love me** to inherit substance; and **I will fill their treasures.** (Proverbs 8:12-21)

The wisdom that God put in Solomon's heart empowered him to build very successful businesses. His businesses helped him to become a ruler of money. Instead of being a slave of money, he became a master of money. This means he did not need to work for money because money was his servant. If you want to become a master of money like Solomon, you first need to seek God earnestly and then pray to Him and ask Him to bless you with the treasures in heaven. One of those treasures is wisdom.

[19] Lay not up for yourselves treasures upon earth, where moth and rust doth corrupt, and where thieves break through and steal: [20] But lay up for yourselves treasures in heaven, where neither moth nor rust doth corrupt, and where thieves do not break through nor steal: [21] For where your treasure is, there will your heart be also. (Matthew 6:19-21)

After praying to God to bless you with the treasures in heaven, believe that you have received those treasures, and He will grant them to you, as long as you do not lose faith. Your faith is the key to answered prayers: "If any of you lack wisdom, let him ask of God, that giveth to all *men* liberally, and upbraideth not; and it shall be given him. But let him ask in faith, nothing wavering. For he that wavereth is like a wave of the sea driven with the wind and tossed. For let not that man think that he shall receive any thing of the Lord" (James 1:5-7).

Whenever you pray to God to ask Him for something, make sure that what you ask is in accordance with His will and the Word of God. Otherwise, He will not grant it to you. Note that there are prayers that require you to do your part. For example, if you pray to God to bless you with a good business, He will send you the right opportunities, people, and miracles to make it easier for that business to manifest in your life, but you have to do the work. God will not do your part, and He will not let you do His part. Remember to end your prayer with the name of Jesus. For example, "In the name of Jesus, Amen." One of the reasons that we end our prayers with the name of Jesus is because Jesus is the Mediator between God and man. He is our High Priest and is the only One holy enough to enter the heavenly sanctuary to reconcile us to God. As sinners, we do not have the authority to enter the heavenly sanctuary, but Jesus has that authority because He is sinless, and He died for our sins. Therefore, through His name, we have access to God, the Father.

The next step to becoming a master of money is to learn important money and business principles and understand them, so you can use them to create wealth and build a successful business. Before we delve into those principles, let us clear up the confusion that it is impossible for a rich man to enter the Kingdom of God. Many Christians and non-

Christians believe that rich people will have a very hard time entering heaven. Because of this belief, they think that being rich is a bad thing. Is it possible for a rich man to enter the Kingdom of God? To find the answer to that question, we need to study Chapter 19 of the Book of Matthew. Let us start by reading verses 16 and 17:

> [16] And, behold, one came and said unto him, **Good** Master, what **good** thing shall I do, that I may have eternal life? [17] And he said unto him, Why callest thou me **good**? *there is* none **good** but one, *that is*, **God**: but if thou wilt enter into life, keep the commandments. (Matthew 19:16–17)

In Matthew 19:16–17, a rich young ruler came to Jesus and asked Him about possessing eternal life. The first sentence he said to Jesus was, "**Good** Master, what **good** thing shall I do, that I may have eternal life?" Did you notice the rich young ruler said **good** twice in that sentence? If we focus on the word good, we can see that the rich young ruler is talking about self-righteousness. The rich young ruler is either ignorant or blinded by pride because he believes he can achieve eternal life by his own good works. This is why he said, "**Good** Master, what **good** thing shall **I do**, that I may have eternal life?" Jesus tried to help the rich young ruler by telling him that no one is good but God. "And he said unto him, Why callest thou me **good**? *there is* none **good** but one, *that is*, **God**: but if thou wilt enter into life, keep the commandments" (Matthew 19:17). Note that Jesus answered the rich young ruler's question with another question. Why? Because Jesus wanted him to understand his own question. That way, he would realize that with man, eternal life is impossible, but with God, anything is possible, even eternal life. Let us read verses 18-22 to learn more about this.

> [18] He saith unto him, Which? Jesus said, Thou shalt do no murder, Thou shalt not commit adultery, Thou shalt not steal, Thou shalt not bear false witness, [19] Honour thy father and *thy* mother: and, Thou shalt love thy neighbour as thyself. [20] The young man saith unto him, All these things have I kept from my youth up: what lack I yet? [21] Jesus said unto him, If thou wilt be perfect, go *and* sell that thou hast, and give to the poor, and thou shalt have treasure in heaven: and come *and* follow me. [22] But when the young man heard that saying, he went away sorrowful: for he had great possessions. (Matthew 19:18-22)

Matthew 19:18-22 reveals that the rich young ruler was blinded by pride and self-righteousness. Evidence of this can be found in verse 20: "The young man saith unto him, All these things have I kept from my youth up: what lack I yet?" Because the rich young ruler was blinded by pride and self-righteousness, he could not hear and see the revelations when Jesus spoke to him. Therefore, Jesus put him to the test in verse 21: "Jesus said unto him, If thou wilt be perfect, go *and* sell that thou hast, and give to the poor, and thou shalt have treasure in heaven: and come *and* follow me." After Jesus said that, the rich young ruler went away sorrowful. Why? Because he loved his possessions more than his neighbors. His act of walking away sorrowful revealed that he failed to keep at least one of the commandments: "Thou shalt love thy neighbour as thyself." After the rich young ruler went away, Jesus revealed some important truths about the Kingdom of God. These truths are important for understanding the question: Is it possible for a rich man to enter the Kingdom of God?

> [23] Then said Jesus unto his disciples, Verily I say unto you, That a rich man shall hardly enter into the kingdom of heaven. [24] And again I say unto you, It is easier for a camel to go through the eye of a needle, than for a **rich** man to enter into the kingdom of God. [25] When his disciples heard *it*, they were exceedingly amazed, saying, Who then can be saved? [26] But Jesus beheld *them*, and said unto them, **With men this is impossible; but with God all things are possible.** (Matthew 19:23–26)

In the previous paragraph, an important word we need to study is rich. In the original text, the word rich is the Greek word πλούσιος (*plousios*), meaning "wealthy, rich, abounding in."[9] The phrase "abounding in" can be found in one of the definitions of rich: "Abounding in valuable ingredients or qualities; as a *rich* odor or flavor; *rich* spices."[10] The word rich also means "self-righteous; abounding, in one's own opinion, with spiritual graces."[11] The rich young ruler was rich in material things, and he was also rich in self-righteousness. It was not his worldly riches that were preventing him from entering the Kingdom of God; it was his self-righteousness and his **trust** in worldly riches. The rich young ruler was so rich in self-righteousness that it blinded him from this truth: "With men this is impossible; but with God all things are possible" (Matthew 19:26). In other words, no amount of self-righteousness can save man from eternal death; only God can save man and give him eternal life.

In Matthew 19:24, Jesus said this important truth: "It is easier for a camel to go through the eye of a needle, than for a rich man to enter into the kingdom of God." This truth is not about being rich in money and material things; if it were, many of God's apostles, prophets, kings, and servants would be lost forever because they were very rich. Furthermore, the Bible would contradict itself if the truth thereof is about being rich in money and material things. One piece of evidence to support the claim that Matthew 19:24 is not talking about being rich in money and material things can be found in Mark 10:24.

> [23] And Jesus looked round about, and saith unto his disciples, How hardly shall they that have riches enter into the kingdom of God! [24] And the disciples were astonished at his words. But Jesus answereth again, and saith unto them, Children, how hard is it for them that **trust** in riches to enter into the kingdom of God! [25] It is easier for a camel to go through the eye of a needle, than for a rich man to enter into the kingdom of God. (Mark 10:23-25)

If we look at the context of the story, we see that the lesson of the story is to rely on the righteousness of God and not our own righteousness. Another lesson of the story is to **trust** God more than any worldly riches, such as money. If we rely on our own righteousness and trust worldly riches more than God, it will be easier for a camel to go through the eye of a needle than for us to enter the Kingdom of God. God's standard is perfection. Every one of us is responsible for living up to His standard, but it is impossible for us to do that because we are born in sin, therefore we cannot live a sinless life. This is why we need a Savior to redeem us from the curse of sin.

Since the fall of man, God knew it was impossible for man to go to heaven through his own good works and righteousness. He also knew that none of His creatures were qualified to redeem man from the curse of sin. The created beings from the angelic kingdom and the animal kingdom could not redeem man because they were lower in rank than man. The only being that was higher in rank than man was God Himself. Therefore, without God's help, man would have to pay the penalty of sin, which is eternal death. For God to redeem man, He would need to be born as a man with innocent blood (free of sin). This is because the blood is what makes atonement for the soul. Without the shedding of blood, there is no remission.

[16] For where a testament *is*, there must also of necessity be the death of the testator. [17] For a testament *is* of force after men are dead: otherwise it is of no strength at all while the testator liveth. [18] Whereupon neither the first *testament* was dedicated without blood. [19] For when Moses had spoken every precept to all the people according to the law, he took the blood of calves and of goats, with water, and scarlet wool, and hyssop, and sprinkled both the book, and all the people, [20] Saying, This *is* the blood of the testament which God hath enjoined

unto you. [21] Moreover he sprinkled with blood both the tabernacle, and all the vessels of the ministry. [22] And almost all things are by the law purged with blood; and **without shedding of blood is no remission**. (Hebrews 9:16–22)

Before God could begin His journey to become the Savior, He needed to become flesh. That way, He could offer Himself as the sacrificial Lamb to take away the sin of the world. To become a man made of flesh and blood, God planted His Seed in the untainted womb of the virgin Mary, allowing His Seed to grow and become a body made of flesh and blood. God's Seed is the Word, and the Word became flesh and was called Jesus (*Yeshua* in Hebrew). "And the Word was made flesh, and dwelt among us, (and we beheld his glory, the glory as of the only begotten of the Father,) full of grace and truth" (John 1:14). This means that Jesus is God in the flesh. "For unto us a child is born, unto us a son is given: and the government shall be upon his shoulder: and his name shall be called Wonderful, Counsellor, **The mighty God**, The everlasting Father, The Prince of Peace" (Isaiah 9:6).

Jesus is the only Man who can save man from eternal death because He is perfect and sinless. Before Jesus paid the price for man's sin by dying on the cross, He took the curse of sin upon His body to be sin for us, so that we might become righteous through Him (2 Corinthians 5:21). "Who his own self bare our sins in his own body on the tree, that we, being dead to sins, should live unto righteousness: by whose stripes ye were healed" (1 Peter 2:24).

Let us turn our attention back to the rich young ruler. On a deeper level, the story about the rich young ruler asking

Jesus about possessing eternal life is a very important story about salvation. The gift of salvation is eternal life. This is the greatest gift from God and is one of the main reasons that Jesus died on the cross. Sin took immortality away from man, but Jesus shed his blood on the cross to make eternal life available to people who trust Him and accept Him as their Lord and Savior. The rich young ruler failed to understand how precious eternal life is. This is why he chose his worldly riches over eternal life.

A man can only make money and enjoy his worldly riches while he is alive. When he is dead, he cannot make any more money and his worldly riches are no longer in his control. Without eternal life, there is no point in having money and riches. Therefore, if you want to be a true master of money, you need to yield to Jesus so He can offer you the gift of eternal life. Before Jesus can offer you this divine gift, you need to confess with your mouth that He is your Lord and Savior and believe in your heart that God raised Him from the dead. "For with the heart man believeth unto righteousness; and with the mouth confession is made unto salvation" (Romans 10:10). If you want to receive the gift of eternal life, say the following prayer earnestly.

> Heavenly Father, I confess that I have sinned and have fallen short of Your glory. I thank You for loving me so much that You sent Your only begotten Son, Jesus, to pay the penalty for my sin. With my mouth, I confess that Jesus, the Christ, is my Lord and Savior, and I believe in my heart that You, the one true God, raised Jesus from the dead. Jesus, I

now invite You to come into my heart and be my Lord and Savior. In the name of Jesus, Amen.

Chapter 4
The Principles of Wealth

In Chapter 3, we explored why wisdom is essential for creating wealth. We also explored important principles on how to become the master of money. One of those principles reveals that it is possible for people who are rich in money to enter the Kingdom of God. Because we now know how to become the master of money, let us explore some important money and business principles. By exploring and studying these principles, you will understand how to apply them to your life, giving you the wisdom to multiply your money. Keep in mind, money cannot be enjoyed without life and freedom, so always value life and freedom more than money.

One of the most important principles related to money is that all the wealth on earth belongs to God. It belongs to Him because He created the earth and everything in it. "Behold, the heaven and the heaven of heavens *is* the LORD's thy God, the earth *also*, with all that therein *is*" (Deuteronomy 10:14). "The silver *is* mine, and the gold *is* mine, saith the LORD of hosts" (Haggai 2:8). Therefore, when you receive money and riches, remember to thank God for allowing you to partake in that wealth. The more you thank God and praise Him, the more He will bless you with good things.

Another important principle related to money is that money is not wealth, strictly speaking. Wealth is the value you create for others.[1] When you create a product or service that is valuable to people, they are more likely to exchange their money for that product or service. Therefore, the money you get from selling your product or service is evidence of your wealth. In general, money can be defined as wealth, but strictly speaking, money and wealth are not the same thing. Because money is evidence of wealth, if you want to be rich, focus on creating wealth. One of the ways to do this is by creating effective solutions for other people's problems. Before creating these solutions, you need to think of them first. Therefore, practice thinking daily and take action to strengthen your creativity, so you can think of effective solutions to change the world. A solution can be a product that helps people overcome a problem. For example, a paper clip is a simple yet useful product for holding sheets of paper together.

If creating a product is not something you like to do, learn about a skill set and practice it to the point where you become a master at it. It is best to choose a skill set that is related to your God-given talent because it will be easier for you to master it. For example, if you are natural at drawing, dedicate a lot of your time and effort to learning a set of skills related to drawing, while at the same time putting that skill set into practice. As you become better at using your skill set, use social media and email platforms to build groups of followers, so that you can promote offers to these groups. An example of an offer is a private art class with a membership fee or a ticket to see you draw in real life. Most people are willing to pay money to see a master perform a skill set, but they are not willing to pay money to see an average person perform the same thing. The more you master performing a skill set or creating a product to improve people's lives, the more people will pay you money to see you perform that skill set or buy that product because they value it more than money.

Let us turn our attention back to creating wealth through effective solutions. Once you think of a solution for helping people overcome a problem, take action to manifest that solution into a product or service. If your solution is a product, build a product-based business to help you sell your product. If your solution is a service, build a service-based business to help you sell your service. Keep in mind that a product-based business has the most potential for making you rich. A service-based business is not as effective for making you rich because the amount of money you can make depends heavily on your time, which is a limited resource. In a sense, you are selling your time. There is only one of you, and you cannot multiply yourself. Furthermore, you only have 24 hours per day to serve others. If you sell a product, you can multiply that product as much as you want. For example, if you sell hats and someone orders 1,000 hats, your business or supplier can fill that order by manufacturing 1,000 hats and shipping them to the customer. You cannot do that in a service-based business, but there are some exceptions. For example, if you open a dance studio, you can multiply your money by charging each dancer a membership fee. However, the number of memberships is limited to the size of the dance studio, and you are still limited to 24 hours per day.

After knowing what type of business you want to build to promote and sell your product or service, the next step is to connect with people who are interested in it. For example, if your product or service helps people sleep better, you should focus on connecting with people who have sleep disorders. It is important to connect with people quickly, so enough of them become aware of your brand in a short amount of time. Remember that quality is important, so focus on the people who will strengthen your brand. One of the best ways to connect with people quickly is through social media. To grow your business quickly, create several social media pages using different social media platforms to inform people about your business and use these pages to promote your brand. It is wise to post both written and video content on your social media daily or weekly. Doing this will increase people's interest in your business and boost sales. Whether you build a product-based business or service-based business, always remember to build your business in a way that pleases God and serves the customers of your business honorably.

An important business principle for generating wealth that you need to remember is that time is not money. One of the reasons is that wealth is measured more in time than money. For example, if it takes you 50 years to make a million dollars, you are not rich by today's standards. If you do the math, the amount of money you make per year will be 20,000 dollars. On the other hand, if it takes you a year to make a million dollars, you will be considered rich. This means that time is not money. However, time plays a big role in determining how much money you can make in a lifetime.

Take note that time is more valuable than money because you can make more money, but you cannot make more time. If you run out of time, you are dead, but if you run out of money, you can always make more money.[2] Even though time is not money, time can help you make more money if you know how to use it effectively. One of the ways to use time effectively is by building a product-based business to multiply your money, reducing the amount of time it takes for you to become rich. On the other hand, an hourly job is ineffective at multiplying your money, preventing you from getting rich quickly. This is because the wage you earn from an hourly job is restricted to an hourly wage.

Most rich people usually do not like to waste time, and they hate sleeping beyond what is necessary. They also hate procrastination. Oversleeping and procrastination are enemies of success because they lead to laziness and waste time. Be aware that one of the enemies of success is oversleeping and not sleeping. Sleeping is beneficial for energy and health, but oversleeping regularly may lead to laziness, depression, weight gain, and other medical conditions.

One of the ways to overcome procrastination is to think about something or do something that ignites the flame of motivation inside you, motivating you to act without procrastination. For me, reading the Bible or listening to inspirational music helps me overcome procrastination. For others, thinking about the future of their loved ones or eliminating distractions in their lives motivates them to act without wasting precious time.

Deep down, everyone knows time is more valuable than money. This truth always reveals itself to people when they have a life-threatening disease. For example, if you contracted a deadly disease and only had a few months to live, but your life could be saved by injecting a very expensive medication into your body, would you be willing to pay a lot of money for that medication, even if it costs one million dollars or more? If people have the money, they will not hesitate to pay for a medication that can save their lives. Even if they do not have the money, they will desperately search for a way to get that money to pay for the medication, so they have more time to live.

Valuing time more than money is an important principle of wealth. Once you understand this principle, learn to manage your time wisely, so you have more time to create wealth. Remember, wealth is the value you create for others. One of the best ways to create wealth is by offering a product or service to improve people's lives. However, if you want more time to enjoy life, offer a product that generates passive income. A print-on-demand book is a great example of a product that generates passive income. Writing a print-on-demand book may not excite most people, but it is one of the best ways to buy back your time, allowing you to have more time to enjoy life. Print on demand (POD) is one of the most efficient ways to distribute books because the books are only printed and shipped after they are ordered. Furthermore, the POD company handles the printing and shipping of the books and customer inquiries. By using print on demand, you do not need to print your books in bulk and store them somewhere, reducing cost and saving time.

Have you ever searched for a book in a bookstore or online only to discover the book is out of print? With POD, there's no such thing. Print on demand publishing keeps your book in an online database and only prints copies of your book as needed, so that your books are available as long as you allow them. Any books you want to publish will remain available as long as you make them as a publisher utilizing print on demand. Whether you are publishing romance novels or political nonfiction, there may come a time when your titles become more sought out or particularly relevant. POD allows your children's children's children—and everyone they know—to have access to your titles long after you have stopped writing and/or publishing.[3]

The process of creating a book involves a lot of thinking, researching, and writing. Because of this, it requires investing many hours of your time to convert your ideas into written content. However, once you are done writing your book, you can get paid for the rest of your life, as long as your book is available for purchase. You write your print-on-demand book once, which generates passive income for the rest of your life. Is that not amazing? There are not many products that generate that kind of passive income. Remember that writing a book is the easy part. The hard part is motivating people to buy your book. Therefore, like building any business, you need to think like a business leader, understand your customers, and have a few tools to promote your book, such as email marketing software and social media pages. Once your email subscribers and social media followers start to grow, you can reach more people, making it easier for you to sell your book.

A subscription website (membership website) is also another great example of a product that generates passive income. Before creating a subscription website, find a niche you like and then learn about that niche while applying what you have learned to your business. By doing this, you will acquire a lot of knowledge and wisdom in relation to that niche. It is wise to choose a niche that is pleasing to God so that He can bless you with more riches. A great feature of a website is that you can use it to sell online courses, which are great for generating passive income. This is done by charging a monthly or yearly fee to access your online courses. You record your online courses once, and they generate passive income for you for the rest of your life, as long as your subscription website is online.

If print-on-demand books or subscription websites do not interest you, there are other products and assets (e.g., rental properties) that are great for generating passive income. A great tool to help you learn more about these products and assets is the Internet. Use this tool to do a thorough investigation on passive income products and assets, so you have a better understanding of which passive income products and assets suit you the most. Products and assets that generate passive income are great for helping you buy back your time. If the idea of buying back your time excites you, you need to learn how to apply automation in your life and business. "Automation is the use of technology to perform tasks with where human input is minimized. This includes enterprise applications such as business process automation (BPA), IT automation, network automation, automating integration between systems, industrial automation such as robotics, and consumer applications such as home automation and more."[4]

Automation simplifies certain tasks by using technology to accomplish those tasks automatically. This frees up labor and saves time and money. Many rich people understand how important automation is for saving time, which is why they create systems to automate tasks, allowing them to have more time to build wealth. Once you understand the power of automation, you can use it to create a system to help you save time and make more money. When you have more money, you can pay other people to work for you or do the chores you do not like, such as shoveling snow or cutting grass, allowing you more time to enjoy life with your loved ones. This is how you can buy back your time and be the master of money. When you are the master of money, money works for you and chases after you, instead of you working for money and chasing after it.

Another way to make money work for you is by investing in financial products, such as bonds and cryptocurrencies (cryptos). The revolutionary technology behind most cryptos is called blockchain. This amazing technology is revolutionizing the financial system by allowing transactions to be processed without the need for a central authority. "A blockchain is a distributed database or ledger shared among a computer network's nodes. They are best known for their crucial role in cryptocurrency systems for maintaining a secure and decentralized record of transactions, but they are not limited to cryptocurrency uses."[5]

Blockchain technology works similarly to an old-fashioned bookkeeping ledger, but instead of containing a handwritten list of entries and calculations, a blockchain contains a digital list of entries and calculations. One of the features that make blockchain technology so revolutionary is its ability to reach consensus automatically, meaning that the consensus algorithm of the blockchain can reach a common agreement on every transaction without relying on a central authority. Because of this, blockchain technology can be used to create a trustless financial system where all transactions are verified automatically without the expensive cost of a traditional financial system.

The first cryptocurrency to harness blockchain technology successfully is called Bitcoin. This means that Bitcoin is the first distributed ledger to achieve full consensus without the need for third parties (e.g., central banks) to validate transactions.[6] A financial system that validates transactions automatically is much more efficient than a financial system that relies on third parties to validate its transactions. The former is more efficient because currency is not being used to pay third parties to validate transactions, allowing more economic energy to stay in the economy, which in turn produces more prosperity. Furthermore, there is less risk of corruption because it is run by computer programs that cannot be bribed.

An important feature of blockchain technology is that it can be used to create decentralized networks. These networks are resilient to censorship, and some are nearly unstoppable. One of the most decentralized networks is the Bitcoin network. The nodes of the Bitcoin network exist in tens of thousands, if not hundreds of thousands, of computers worldwide. A node, or more specifically a full node, is a computer program that validates transactions and stores the entire blockchain data of the Bitcoin network. In other words, each full node contains the exact copy of the entire blockchain data, making it nearly impossible to destroy the Bitcoin network. Even if a government or an organization can destroy 99 percent of the Bitcoin nodes, if one computer still contains a full node, it can be used to reboot the Bitcoin network without any loss of data and with little effort. To a large extent, this makes the Bitcoin network indestructible and immune to censorship. Keep in mind that blockchain is a technology, and like any technology, it can be used for good or evil purposes. Therefore, it is important that we support cryptocurrencies (cryptos) and blockchain companies that care about our freedom, prosperity, and privacy.

In the financial world, blockchain technology increases automation and reduces the need for central authorities (e.g., banks) to lend currency and record and validate transactions. Because of this, the crypto space is full of services that are effective for generating passive income. Staking and yield farming are two of the most popular ways of generating passive income in the crypto space. "Staking cryptocurrency means locking up coins to maintain the security of a blockchain network and earning rewards in return,"[7] and "yield farming is the practice of staking or lending crypto assets in order to generate high returns or rewards in the form of additional cryptocurrency."[8] Staking is usually less risky than yield farming; however, the annual percentage yield (APY) or annual percentage rate (APR) for yield farming is generally higher than staking. Some yield farming platforms offer 20 percent APY/APR or more.

One of my favorite cryptos to stake is Cardano (ADA). The reason is that Cardano allows me to stake its coins (called ADA) without a lockup period. Most cryptos require a lockup period to access their staking rewards. In other words, you cannot access and transfer your cryptos until the lockup period is over.

If done correctly, crypto staking can help you establish multiple passive income streams. The staking APY/APR, which is the interest you earn by staking your cryptos, is the feature that allows you to earn passive income, which you can use to pay expenses (e.g., utility bills and grocery) without sacrificing the principal (the original cryptos that you staked). This means that the principal will not run out, and therefore, you do not need to worry about not having enough currency to pay expenses, as long as you stake your cryptos safely and responsibly.

Besides crypto staking and yield farming, another way to generate passive income in the crypto space is through crypto lending platforms. "Crypto lending is the process of depositing cryptocurrency that is lent out to borrowers in return for regular interest payments. Payments are made in the form of the cryptocurrency that is deposited typically and compounded on a daily, weekly, or monthly basis."[9] In a way, crypto lending allows people to be their own banks. Some crypto lending platforms are decentralized, meaning that they allow people to lend out their cryptos to borrowers without intermediaries. These crypto lending platforms are also permissionless, meaning anyone can freely join and use the platforms without obtaining permission, approval, or authorization.[10]

Before the invention of crypto lending platforms, starting a banking business to lend and borrow currency was expensive and required a lot of legal paperwork. With the rise of blockchain technology and crypto lending platforms, anyone can start a banking business by lending their cryptos to borrowers, allowing them to generate passive income without the expensive cost of traditional banking. This levels the playing field and gives ordinary people the means to lend currency to borrowers anywhere in the world. This new way of lending currency is a threat to the central bankers and their banking empires, which is why they have been taking actions to destroy many cryptos, especially decentralized cryptos. Take note that investing in cryptos is risky and requires responsibility because the crypto space is still new and very volatile. The good news is that with patience, knowledge, and wisdom, investing in cryptos can make you a millionaire faster than any other investment.

Let us explore more business principles for building wealth. An important business principle that is often ignored by many business owners is the principle of loving people more than money. The reason that money has value is because people agree to use it as a medium of exchange. Furthermore, money represents people's labor (energy). Therefore, without people using money as a medium of exchange, money becomes worthless and useless. Money by itself has no value because it needs people to give it value. Because of this, it is important to love people more than money. Even better, always put God and people above money. It is fine to like money, but it is not wise to love money. Why? Because the love of money is the root of all evil. Understanding the business principle of loving people more than money will inspire you to work harder to satisfy your customers and pay your employees well, creating a strong foundation for your business to grow and prosper. As your business continues to prosper, it will bring more riches into your life.

There are two words we need to ponder from the previous paragraph: **rich** and **money**. Many people associate these two words with evil, yet they like to use money to buy material things to make them feel happy or rich. Their lack of understanding the two words thereof manifests confusion and disorder in their lives, making it harder for them to become rich. If you want to become rich, one of the first things you need to do is change the way you think by believing and accepting the idea that being rich is a good thing. Furthermore, stop thinking that rich people are evil. Some rich people like to use money to control the world by bribing politicians and using them to enslave the people of the world, but most rich people do not have that kind of evil desire.

Another thing you need to do to become rich is to protect your mind from the idea that money is evil. Money itself is not evil. It is the **love** of money that gives rise to evil deeds. When people love money, they will eventually love it more than God, transforming money into an idol. Whenever anyone puts money above God, it always leads to greed, death, and destruction. People who love money more than God will never taste true riches because these riches are heavenly riches. Once you become rich, do not forget the true source of your wealth, which is God. No matter how much wealth you have acquired, do not turn away from the LORD God. Always remember that you are rich because of His grace and blessings, and you cannot achieve anything without Him. "I am the vine, ye *are* the branches: He that abideth in me, and I in him, the same bringeth forth much fruit: for without me ye can do nothing" (John 15:5). Also, do not forget how your life was when you were poor, so you can avoid the mistake of looking down on poor people. Always remember that being rich does not make you better than other people.

Many poor people hate rich people because they believe the reason they are poor is because rich people are hoarding all the wealth.[11] If you want to be rich, do not believe in that lie. Yes, some rich people only care about themselves and their wealth, but most rich people are not like that. The idea that there is not enough money for everyone is a lie. The scarcity of money is artificially created by central banks to create the illusion that money is scarce. In reality, there is more than enough money for everyone. This is because the amount of money we make in life is in direct proportion to our resourcefulness.[12] Furthermore, on a grand scale, money represents the economic energy of mankind. The resourcefulness and economic energy of mankind is unlimited. Because of this, there is more than enough money for everyone. Once you understand that the scarcity of money is an illusion, you will know that poor people are poor because they lack the knowledge and wisdom to build wealth.

A crucial reason that poor people are poor is because they do not understand the purpose of money. In general, poor people believe that the purpose of money is for paying bills and buying things.[13] This belief is one of the main reasons that they are poor. Generally speaking, middle-class people's perspective of money is similar to that of poor people, with the additional belief that the purpose of money is to create and maintain good credit, so they can borrow money to buy more things they cannot afford.[14] In general, rich people believe that the purpose of money is to help them make more money. This belief inspires them to find ways to multiply their money through investments, businesses, etc. Rich people are not afraid to embrace new opportunities and are willing to take financial risks. Poor and middle-class people do not like to take financial risks, and they prefer something that guarantees them money over opportunity.

Another reason that poor people are poor is because they are afraid of failure. Their fear of failure is so strong that it prevents them from taking action to make their lives better. In other words, they would rather be poor than face the embarrassment of failure. Unlike poor people, rich people see failures as opportunities for learning lessons. These lessons make them wiser and help them think of new ideas to overcome their failures, making it easier for them to achieve success. Learning lessons from failures is great for improving your perseverance skills, which are important for helping you to accomplish your goals and become successful in life.

In the Body of Christ, many Christians struggle financially because they have been conditioned by the mainstream media and the education system to think like poor people. Some Christians even believe that money is evil. Many Christians do not realize that all the riches on earth belong to their Lord Jesus Christ. The riches thereof are supposed to be in the hands of the children of God, not the children of Satan. If you are a Christian, think about this question: would Jesus want His riches to be in the hands of the children of God or the children of Satan? Because many Christians think like poor people, it allows Satan and his minions to steal the riches on earth to finance his kingdom of darkness, causing death, misery, and destruction to manifest all over the earth. To prevent this, the children of God need to learn how to be rich, so they can take back the riches that were stolen by Satan and use them to finance God's kingdom on earth.

Rich people know that communication and creativity are two of the most important skills for building wealth. Communication skills are great for negotiating deals and inspiring people to buy products. As for creativity skills, they are great for stimulating the mind to think of creative solutions for helping people overcome problems. Because communication and creativity skills are important for building wealth, many rich people focus their time and energy on improving and applying those skills. Therefore, they prefer to hire others to do the implementation work. The combination of communication and creativity skills helps rich people to create great offers, which are crucial for amassing large amounts of wealth. An offer is something you can sell for an **unlimited** amount of time. Many products can be used to create offers. One of them is a book. Books are great for creating offers because they can be sold for an unlimited amount of time. An author who owns the copyright of a book can create an offer for readers to buy copies of his book. Even after all the copies are sold, he can still offer the same offer or create a new offer to sell copies of the same book.

An important principle for building wealth that you need to remember is getting rich quickly. Keep in mind that this is not referring to getting rich through get-rich-quick schemes and other deceitful methods. Getting rich quickly is important for building wealth because the sooner you have more money, the sooner you can use that money to multiply your wealth. This prevents you from using too much of your precious time to work for money. Time is not something you can afford to waste because you only have a limited amount of time to achieve success before your body returns to dust. The sooner you become rich, the sooner you will have more time to enjoy life. That does not mean you cannot enjoy life as a poor person. However, as a poor person, you are more limited in what you can do because nearly everything on earth costs money.

After getting rich quickly, it is important to protect your wealth by investing in investments that multiply money slowly, such as real estate, gold (bullion, ETFs, etc.), and crypto staking. For example, putting one million dollars' worth of cryptos in a crypto staking program with a five percent annual percentage yield (APY) will make you about 50,000 dollars per year on the interest alone. Some crypto staking programs offer more than ten percent APY! When staking cryptos for the long term, it is usually best to stake stablecoins because they are not volatile. The goal is to make money quickly and invest some of that money in low-risk investments that multiply money slowly, so that the interest generated from those investments will eventually surpass your income. If you implement this strategy correctly, you will not have to worry about running out of money. This is one of the ways you can build great wealth and achieve financial freedom.

Most people do not have one hundred thousand dollars or one million dollars to invest in investments to multiply their money, so if you fall into that category, you will need to acquire knowledge on how to grow your money. Furthermore, you will need to apply that knowledge in your life to gain the wisdom to become the master of your money. This chapter contains a lot of knowledge to help you grow your money, so it is important that you study this chapter thoroughly. With that being said, this chapter does not have all the answers, so you will need to seek knowledge from other sources to gain more wisdom and grow your wealth. At the beginning of your journey to amass wealth, remember that one of the first steps to growing your wealth is to acquire the habit of paying some of the money you earn to yourself. In other words, every time you get paid, save some money for investments.

> Every gold piece you save is a slave to work for you. Every copper it earns is its child that also can earn for you. If you would become wealthy, then what you save must earn, and its children must earn, that all may help to give to you the abundance you crave. [...] Wealth, like a tree, grows from a tiny seed. The first copper you save is the seed from which your tree of wealth shall grow. The sooner you plant that seed the sooner shall the tree grow. And the more faithfully you nourish and water that tree with consistent savings, the sooner may you bask in contentment beneath its shade.[15]

Most people know that saving money is an important principle of wealth. However, many do not realize that giving money is also important. Every time you donate to a charity or give money to others generously, you sow a good seed. Furthermore, your charitable act pleases God and brings Him joy, motivating Him to bless you with riches. "But this *I say*, He which soweth sparingly shall reap also sparingly; and he which soweth bountifully shall reap also bountifully. Every man according as he purposeth in his heart, *so let him give*; not grudgingly, or of necessity: for God loveth a cheerful giver" (2 Corinthians 9:6–7).

Heed these words: with great wealth comes great responsibility. Having a lot of money and riches is a blessing, but it can also be a curse. The curse of money can manifest in your life when you are not in control of the desires of your flesh. Consequently, money can amplify those desires, meaning that money makes it easier for you to buy things to exacerbate the desires of your flesh. For example, a poor man who likes to drink alcohol will not be able to buy as much alcohol to drink as a rich man, hindering the poor man from exacerbating his drinking problems. On the other hand, the rich man has money to buy as much alcohol as he wants, creating the environment for alcohol-related problems to manifest in his life.

The fall of King Solomon is a great example of what the desires of the flesh and the curse of money can do to rich people. Solomon fell from God's grace because of his desire to marry many women, including women from foreign nations who worshiped pagan gods. God had warned the children of Israel not to intermarry with the people of those foreign nations, but Solomon did not listen to God's warning.

> [1] But king Solomon loved many strange women,
> together with the daughter of Pharaoh, women of the
> Moabites, Ammonites, Edomites, Zidonians, *and*
> Hittites; [2] Of the nations *concerning* which the Lord
> said unto the children of Israel, Ye shall not go in to
> them, neither shall they come in unto you: *for* surely
> they will turn away your heart after their gods:
> Solomon clave unto these in love. [3] And he had
> seven hundred wives, princesses, and three hundred
> concubines: and his wives turned away his heart. [4]
> For it came to pass, when Solomon was old, *that* his
> wives turned away his heart after other gods: and his
> heart was not perfect with the Lord his God, as *was*
> the heart of David his father. (1 Kings 11:1-4)

When Solomon allowed his foreign wives to turn away his
heart from God, it corrupted his wisdom. Shortly after, his life
went downhill, and he lost much of his riches and honor.
Solomon destroyed his life by listening to his wives instead of
the wisdom of God. If we turn away our hearts from God and
do not listen to His wisdom, we will meet a similar fate. The
fall of King Solomon reveals that no matter how wise, rich,
and successful a man becomes, he is nothing without the
wisdom of God.

> [9] And the Lord was angry with Solomon, because his
> heart was turned from the Lord God of Israel, which
> had appeared unto him twice, [10] And had
> commanded him concerning this thing, that he
> should not go after other gods: but he kept not that

which the LORD commanded. [11] Wherefore the LORD said unto Solomon, Forasmuch as this is done of thee, and thou hast not kept my covenant and my statutes, which I have commanded thee, I will surely rend the kingdom from thee, and will give it to thy servant. [12] Notwithstanding in thy days I will not do it for David thy father's sake: *but* I will rend it out of the hand of thy son. (1 Kings 11:9–12)

Remember these words: with the wisdom of God comes life, honor, authority, wealth, and riches. Because of this, it is important that you seek the Kingdom of God rather than chase after the things of the world. This means that you need to seek the love and wisdom of God with all your heart, so you can yield to Him and acknowledge Him as the sovereign King of your life. By doing this, God becomes your Father and protects you like a father protects his child. God loves all His children and knows the desires of their hearts. He also knows what is best for them because He sees how their choices will affect their lives in the future. Therefore, like any loving father, He disciplines His children and shows them the path that brings the most joy and fulfillment into their hearts.

When you submit to God and make Him the Ruler over your life, He is willing to make you the king over an assignment, meaning "a position of responsibility, post of duty, or the like, to which one is appointed."[16] God wants to make you the ruler over an assignment because He gave man dominion over all the earth. The evidence of this can be found in Genesis 1:26: "And God said, Let us make man in our image, after our likeness: and let them have **dominion** over the fish of the sea, and over the fowl of the air, and over the cattle, and **over all the earth**, and over every creeping thing that creepeth upon the earth." One of the definitions of dominion is "sovereign or supreme authority; the power of governing and controlling."[17] Throughout the Bible, God gave kings many assignments. One of His most important assignments was given to Adam, which was to rule over all the earth. Another one was assigned to King Solomon, which was to rule over Israel.

It is an honor to be appointed by God to be the king over an assignment. God gives heavenly riches to those who serve Him and supplies all the things they need to accomplish their assignments: as long as they serve God faithfully and righteously, He will bless them with valuable gifts (e.g., wisdom, food, money, etc.), similar to how a father blesses his child with valuable gifts when he does good deeds. This is one of the deeper meanings of Matthew 6:33: "But seek ye first the kingdom of God, and his righteousness; and all these things shall be added unto you."

God usually gives people assignments according to their skills and talents. For example, God may use people with musical skills to create inspirational songs to uplift people's souls. For people with business skills, He may use them to build businesses to empower people and help the poor rise out of poverty. If God makes you the king over an assignment, it is wise to do it in a way that pleases God and serve the people related to that assignment with love, honor, and integrity.[18] In business, serving people with love, honor, and integrity is very important for success. It is like building a house on a rock. This is why creating a business with the foundation to serve people with love, honor, and integrity is important. Building this type of business will make you feel more joyful and fulfilled in life. Furthermore, the Law of Seedtime and Harvest will manifest many good harvests in your life. Let us revisit Chapter 1 to remind us about how this law works:

> To understand the Law of Seedtime and Harvest, it is essential to know that thoughts and words are spiritual seeds. However, spoken words act as the vessels that carry these thoughts (spiritual seeds) into the external world. Every time you speak words, you cast your thoughts/seeds into the external world. Therefore, whenever you speak words, you sow (plant) seeds. Once you understand this, it becomes clear that a good harvest is the result of sowing good seeds. Conversely, sowing bad seeds yields a bad harvest, manifesting unpleasant and painful experiences in your life.

It is important to understand that the Law of Seedtime and Harvest also applies to actions. Therefore, your words and actions determine the type of harvest you reap. If you want more wealth to manifest in your life, speak words related to wealth, prosperity, and abundance; you also need to take the right actions to support these words. This method of manifesting a good harvest into your life also applies to building a successful business. This is why building a business to serve people with love, honor, and integrity is important. The key is to serve people, not money. Money is the byproduct of the wealth people create with their will and energy. By building a business to serve people, it attracts not only wealth but also money into your business. Once you understand this business model and apply it to your life, the garden or field where you sow your seeds (words and actions) is seeded with many good seeds. As a result, when harvesttime comes, you will reap a harvest of abundance, manifesting wealth and joy into your life.

Living a joyful and fulfilling life is a life that most people want to have, but many of them fail to manifest it into reality because they rely too much on money to fill the emptiness in their hearts. This void cannot be filled by the things of the world. It can only be filled by the love of God through Jesus Christ. The love of God cannot be truly known without Jesus. This is because Jesus is the Mediator between God and man. In other words, through Jesus, you have access to God, the Father. When you earnestly confess with your mouth that Jesus is the Lord of your life, He comes into your heart and baptizes you with the Holy Spirit. Through the power of the Holy Spirit, your heart starts to transform from a heart of stone into a heart of flesh, allowing you to receive the love of God. If you want God to give you a new heart, repent of your sins and say the following prayer earnestly.

> Dear God, I confess with my mouth that Jesus, the Christ, is my Lord and Savior, and I believe in my heart that You, the one true God, raised Jesus from the dead. Jesus, I now invite You to come into my heart and be my Lord and Savior. In the name of Jesus, Amen.

If you earnestly said that prayer, you are no longer a sinner. This does not mean you are free from sinful thoughts and desires while living on earth. It also does not mean you cannot sin. What it means is that the blood of Jesus has washed away your sins. Therefore, as long as you understand that it is His blood that frees you from sin and not your own good works, the law cannot legally judge you as a sinner. This is the law of God that gives man the knowledge of sin, but it also accuses man of being a sinner. In addition, the law has the authority to condemn man to death and eternal punishment in hell for committing sin. This is why the Bible refers to the law as the letter (of legally written code) that kills (2 Corinthians 3:6).

It is crucial to remember that the law is devoid of mercy, forgiveness, and life, which is why it looks to the letter of the law instead of the spirit. Furthermore, it enforces the principle of justice known as "an eye for an eye," which requires punishment equal in kind to the offense. The law focuses on legalism and is written for the unregenerate man, also known as the natural man or the fallen man, who only sees the external meanings of the law because he is incapable of interpreting and knowing spiritual truths. The law thereof is the main law that rules over the legal system, which is a system that deals with the spiritually dead. Maybe this is why most judges of the legal system wear a black robe. The color black represents sin and death. The legal system also administers man-made laws, but these laws do not supersede the law because it is written by God.

Since the fall of Adam and Eve, all men, women, and children have been born in sin and therefore are sinners. They are also spiritually dead, except the ones who are born again spiritually. Because they are sinners and spiritually dead, they fall under the jurisdiction of the law and the legal system.

The evidence that all men, women, and children are spiritually dead can be found in 1 Corinthians 15:22: "For as in Adam all die, even so in Christ shall all be made alive." Because all men, women, and children are spiritually dead, they are debtors, also known as sinners (slaves of sin/debt). Some of the evidence that supports the previous statement can be found in the definition of sin, debt, and debtor, and in Romans 5:12.

> **Sin:** The voluntary departure of a moral agent from a known rule of rectitude or duty, prescribed by God; any voluntary transgression of the divine law, or violation of a divine command; a wicked act; iniquity.[19]

> **Debt:** In scripture, **sin**; trespass; guilt; crime; that which renders liable to punishment.[20]

> **Debtor:** One who is guilty of a trespass or sin; a sinner.[21]

> **Romans 5:12:** Wherefore, as by one man sin entered into the world, and **death by sin**; and so death passed upon all men, for that all have sinned:

According to the previous definitions, all sinners are debtors who are slaves of debt (one of the fruits of sin). Since sinners are slaves of sin/debt, they cannot become truly wealthy because they have no eternal life and cannot access God's heavenly treasures. This is why it is essential to learn about salvation, so you know how to receive the gift of eternal life, which is God's most valuable treasure. There is **only one way** you can receive the gift of eternal life: through the blood of

Jesus. Evidence of this can be found in studying the law. According to the law, the forgiveness of sin requires the shedding of blood. This is because committing sin is equivalent to committing murder. Hence, Romans 6:23: "For the wages of sin *is* **death**; but the gift of God *is* eternal life through Jesus Christ our Lord." Because committing sin is equivalent to committing murder, freeing a sinner requires the shedding of blood: a life for a life.

> [16] For where a testament *is*, there must also of necessity be the death of the testator. [17] For a testament *is* of force after men are dead: otherwise it is of no strength at all while the testator liveth. [18] Whereupon neither the first *testament* was dedicated without blood. [19] For when Moses had spoken every precept to all the people according to the law, he took the blood of calves and of goats, with water, and scarlet wool, and hyssop, and sprinkled both the book, and all the people, [20] Saying, This *is* the blood of the testament which God hath enjoined unto you. [21] Moreover he sprinkled with blood both the tabernacle, and all the vessels of the ministry. [22] And almost all things are by the law purged with blood; and **without shedding of blood is no remission.** (Hebrews 9:16-22)

An important word we need to study in the previous paragraph is testament. Understanding this word on a deeper level will help us comprehend how we can access the riches of heaven and earth. One of the definitions of testament is "a **will**, especially one that relates to the disposition of one's personal property."[22] The word testament is defined by *A Dictionary of Law* using these words: "Written or oral instructions, properly 'witnessed' and authenticated, according to the pleasure of the deceased, for the disposition of his effects. [...] Originally, a 'testament' concerned personalty only, and a 'devise' or 'will' realty. Later, the general expression for an instrument embracing either or both species of property was 'last will and testament,' or simply a 'will.' The terms are now interchanged."[23] Here are two more important definitions of testament:

> 1. A solemn authentic instrument in writing, by which a person **declares his will** as to the disposal of his estate and effects after his death. This is otherwise called a **will**. A *testament* to be valid, must be made when the testator is of sound mind, and it must be subscribed, witnessed and published in such manner as the law prescribes.[24]

> 2. The name of each general division of the canonical books of the sacred Scriptures; as the Old Testament; the New Testament. The name is equivalent to **covenant**, and in our use of it, we apply it to the books which contain the old and new dispensations; that of Moses, and that of Jesus Christ.[25]

Based on the definitions of testament, a testament is a will. It is also a covenant, meaning "a mutual consent or agreement of two or more persons, to do or to forbear some act or thing; a contract; stipulation."[26] Note that a testament is only valid after the testator's death (the one who makes the will). Before

Jesus died on the cross, He left a will for His children (the children of God). His will is recorded in the New Testament. Remember, the word testament means "will." In the New Testament, Jesus declared many types of good news. One of them is the gift of eternal life. Another one is the restoration of man's inheritance (e.g., dominion over all the earth) that Adam lost when he committed sin in the Garden of Eden.

Jesus is the Heir of all things (Hebrews 1:2). Before He ascended to heaven, He left personal and universal gifts for His heirs. The heirs thereof are the children of God, also called the sons of God, heirs of God, and joint-heirs with Christ. They are the people who have received sonship by confessing with their mouths that Jesus is their Lord and Savior and believing in their hearts that God raised Him from the dead.

> [14] For as many as are led by the Spirit of God, they are **the sons of God**. [15] For ye have not received the spirit of bondage again to fear; but ye have received the Spirit of adoption, whereby we cry, Abba, Father. [16] The Spirit itself beareth witness with our spirit, that we are **the children of God**: [17] And if children, then heirs; **heirs of God**, and **joint-heirs with Christ**; if so be that we suffer with *him*, that we may be also glorified together. (Romans 8:14-17)

If you have earnestly confessed with your mouth that Jesus is your Lord and Savior and believe in your heart that God raised Him from the dead, you are a child and heir of God. This means that when Jesus returns to earth to rule over it, you will rule along with Him. Furthermore, when you enter

His eternal kingdom, you will jointly possess all that He possesses. In other words, that which Christ inherits, you also inherit through Him.[27] This is the great secret to eternal wealth and how you become wealthy for eternity! As for the personal gifts that Jesus left for you, many clues to help you find those gifts are in the Bible. Other clues can be found through prayers. Your personal gifts may be different from others, so when reading the Bible, ask the Holy Spirit to reveal revelations about your gifts to you. Take note that the Lord blesses those who are humble. Therefore, humble yourself in the sight of the Lord, and He will bless you with many gifts.

It is important to remember that the greatest gift from God, the Father, is the gift of eternal life through Jesus Christ. The revelations of this divine gift are recorded in the Bible, which consists of stories, not fables and myths but true stories, written by authors who were under the influence and guidance of the Holy Spirit. The Bible is the Word of God and contains the instructions on receiving the gift of eternal life, which is more precious than all the riches of the world. Why is eternal life so precious? With eternal life comes the joy of experiencing the glorious Kingdom of God, which is eternal and full of riches that are beyond imagination.

One of the most important revelations for helping us understand why eternal life is so precious is the revelation of how man has fallen from grace and is imprisoned in a fallen world that he cannot escape. In all of creation, no creature was able to save man from the curse of sin because they did not meet the criteria. This is because man was the only creature created in the image and likeness of God, making man the highest created being, even higher than angels.

Therefore, no creature was worthy and valuable enough to pay the penalty for man's sin. The only being higher than man was God Himself.

The Bible reveals that God loved us so much that He (the Word) came in the flesh through the virgin Mary, allowing Him to walk on earth in the form of man, so He (Jesus, the only begotten Son of God) could bear our sins and die in our place, saving us from the curse of sin legally. Jesus defeated death for us by dying for our sins, giving us access to the gift of eternal life. That is how much He loves us. Jesus' sacrificial and generous acts reveal that He is the perfect radiance of God's glory and love and the perfect example of how we should live as children of the Most High God.

> [16] For God so loved the world, that he gave his only begotten Son, that whosoever believeth in him should not perish, but have everlasting life. (John 3:16)

References

Chapter 1

1. Bible Hub. *Kakos.*
    https://biblehub.com/greek/2556.htm
2. Online Etymology Dictionary. *Evil.*
    https://www.etymonline.com/word/evil
3. American Dictionary of the English Language
    (1828). *Devil.*
    https://webstersdictionary1828.com/Dictionary/devil
4. American Dictionary of the English Language
    (1828). *Live.*
    https://webstersdictionary1828.com/Dictionary/live
5. Dictionary. *Live.*
    https://www.dictionary.com/browse/live
6. Dictionary. *Life.*
    https://www.dictionary.com/browse/life
7. American Dictionary of the English Language
    (1828). *Life.*
    https://webstersdictionary1828.com/Dictionary/life

8. Dictionary. *Death.*
   https://www.dictionary.com/browse/death
9. American Dictionary of the English Language
   (1828). *Death.*
   https://webstersdictionary1828.com/Dictionary/death
10. Dictionary. *Evil.*
    https://www.dictionary.com/browse/evil
11. American Dictionary of the English Language
    (1828). *Evil.*
    https://webstersdictionary1828.com/Dictionary/evil
12. Dictionary. *Good.*
    https://www.dictionary.com/browse/good
13. Online Etymology Dictionary. *Good.*
    https://www.etymonline.com/word/good
14. Got Questions. *Why Does Isaiah 45:7 Say That God
    Created Evil?* https://www.gotquestions.org/Isaiah-45-
    7.html
15. Bible Study Tools. *Ra.*
    https://www.biblestudytools.com/lexicons/hebrew/nas
    /ra.html
16. YouTube. *Money Follow$ Ma$tery - Easy Money -
    Myron Golden Ph.D.*
    https://www.youtube.com/watch?v=38SpmVwUOEE
17. The Gospel Coalition. *Original Sin.*
    https://www.thegospelcoalition.org/essay/original-sin/
18. Online Etymology Dictionary. *Currency.*
    https://www.etymonline.com/word/currency
19. Dictionary. *Current.*
    https://www.dictionary.com/browse/current

20. Dictionary. *Electrolyte.*
https://www.dictionary.com/browse/electrolyte
21. Dictionary. *Bank.*
https://www.dictionary.com/browse/bank
22. Black, Henry C. *Black's Law Dictionary (Fourth Edition).* West Publishing Co. St. Paul, MN. 1968.
23. Dictionary. *River.*
https://dictionary.cambridge.org/us/dictionary/english/river
24. Merriam-Webster. *Bank.* https://www.merriam-webster.com/dictionary/bank
25. Cambridge Dictionary. *Riverbank.*
https://dictionary.cambridge.org/us/dictionary/english/riverbank
26. Dictionary. *Liquidate.*
https://www.dictionary.com/browse/liquidate
27. Dictionary. *Corpse.*
https://www.dictionary.com/browse/corpse

Chapter 2

1. YouTube. *Money vs Currency - Hidden Secrets of Money Episode 1 - Mike Maloney.*
https://www.youtube.com/watch?v=DyV0OfU3-FU
2. Black, Henry C. *Black's Law Dictionary (Seventh Edition).* West Group. St. Paul, MN. 1999.
3. Dictionary. *Inflation.*
https://www.dictionary.com/browse/inflation
4. YouTube. *Bank Crisis & Inflation: The Biggest Scam in the History of Mankind - Hidden Secrets of*

Money Ep 4.
https://www.youtube.com/watch?v=iFDe5kUUyT0

5. Britannica. *Fiat Money.*
https://www.britannica.com/money/fiat-money

6. Dictionary. *Fiat.*
https://www.dictionary.com/browse/fiat

7. Money. *What Is Fiat Money?*
https://money.com/what-is-fiat-money/

8. Dictionary. *Bond.*
https://www.dictionary.com/browse/bond

9. YouTube. *Bank Crisis & Inflation: The Biggest Scam in the History of Mankind - Hidden Secrets of Money Ep 4.*
https://www.youtube.com/watch?v=iFDe5kUUyT0

10. YouTube. *Bank Crisis & Inflation: The Biggest Scam in the History of Mankind - Hidden Secrets of Money Ep 4.*
https://www.youtube.com/watch?v=iFDe5kUUyT0

11. Investopedia. *What Are Open Market Operations (OMOs), and How Do They Work?*
https://www.investopedia.com/terms/o/openmarketo perations.asp

12. American Dictionary of the English Language (1828). *Debt.*
https://webstersdictionary1828.com/Dictionary/debt

13. American Dictionary of the English Language (1828). *Debt.*
https://webstersdictionary1828.com/Dictionary/debt

14. Dictionary. *Bondage.*
https://www.dictionary.com/browse/bondage

15. Dictionary. *Bondage.*
https://www.dictionary.com/browse/bondage
16. IRS. *The Agency, Its Mission and Statutory Authority.* https://www.irs.gov/about-irs/the-agency-its-mission-and-statutory-authority
17. The Balance. *What Is the Internal Revenue Service (IRS)?* https://www.thebalancemoney.com/the-internal-revenue-service-3193097
18. Justia U.S. Supreme Court. *Donaldson v. United States, 400 U.S. 517 (1971).*
https://supreme.justia.com/cases/federal/us/400/517/
19. Investopedia. *Fractional Reserve Banking: What It Is and How It Works.*
https://www.investopedia.com/terms/f/fractionalreservebanking.asp
20. Online Etymology Dictionary. *Economy.*
https://www.etymonline.com/word/economy
21. Dictionary. *Economy.*
https://www.dictionary.com/browse/economy
22. American Dictionary of the English Language (1828). *Economy.*
https://webstersdictionary1828.com/Dictionary/economy
23. Dictionary. *Prudent.*
https://www.dictionary.com/browse/prudent
24. The Lawful Path. *Silent Weapons for Quiet Wars.*
http://www.lawfulpath.com
25. The Lawful Path. *Silent Weapons for Quiet Wars.*
http://www.lawfulpath.com

26. Britannica. *Fiat Money.*
https://www.britannica.com/money/fiat-money
27. AZ Quotes. *Thomas Jefferson Quotes.*
https://www.azquotes.com/quote/709777

Chapter 3

1. American Dictionary of the English Language (1828). *Wisdom.*
https://webstersdictionary1828.com/Dictionary/wisdo m
2. American Dictionary of the English Language (1828). *Knowledge.*
https://webstersdictionary1828.com/Dictionary/know ledge
3. Dictionary. *Knowledge.*
https://www.dictionary.com/browse/knowledge
4. American Dictionary of the English Language (1828). *Understanding.*
https://webstersdictionary1828.com/Dictionary/unde rstanding
5. American Dictionary of the English Language (1828). *Understanding.*
https://webstersdictionary1828.com/Dictionary/unde rstanding
6. YouTube. *Money Follow$ Ma$tery - Easy Money - Myron Golden Ph.D.*
https://www.youtube.com/watch?v=38SpmVwUOEE
7. Merriam-Webster. Assimilate. https://www.merriam-webster.com/dictionary/assimilate

8. Got Questions. *How Is the Fear of the Lord the Beginning of Wisdom?*
https://www.gotquestions.org/fear-Lord-beginning-wisdom.html

9. Bible Hub. *Plousios.*
https://biblehub.com/greek/4145.htm

10. American Dictionary of the English Language (1828). *Rich.*
https://webstersdictionary1828.com/Dictionary/rich

11. American Dictionary of the English Language (1828). *Rich.*
https://webstersdictionary1828.com/Dictionary/rich

Chapter 4

1. YouTube. *How to Make, Manage, and Multiply Wealth.*
https://www.youtube.com/watch?v=KY2bAlZIpXs

2. YouTube. *How Rich People Think About Money (Psychology of Money).*
https://www.youtube.com/watch?v=rdctz6zSMKw

3. IngramSpark. *Benefits of Print on Demand for Indie Publishers.* https://www.ingramspark.com/blog/print-on-demand-for-indie-publishers

4. IBM. *What Is Automation?*
https://www.ibm.com/topics/automation

5. Investopedia. *Blockchain Facts: What Is It, How It Works, and How It Can Be Used.*
https://www.investopedia.com/terms/b/blockchain.asp

6. YouTube. *From Bitcoin to HBAR - Hedera Hashgraph Documentary.*
   https://www.youtube.com/watch?v=SF362xxcfdk
7. Binance Academy. *What Is Crypto Staking and How Does It Work?*
   https://academy.binance.com/en/articles/what-is-staking
8. CoinMarketCap. *What Is Yield Farming?*
   https://coinmarketcap.com/academy/article/what-is-yield-farming
9. Investopedia. *Crypto Lending: What It Is, How It Works, Types.* https://www.investopedia.com/crypto-lending-5443191
10. Cryptopedia. *What Does Permissionless Mean?*
    https://www.gemini.com/cryptopedia/what-is-permissionless-crypto-permissionlessness-blockchain
11. YouTube. *A Simple Formula to Make Millions.*
    https://www.youtube.com/watch?v=nLlf6hg4H0Q
12. YouTube. *A Simple Formula to Make Millions.*
    https://www.youtube.com/watch?v=nLlf6hg4H0Q
13. YouTube. *How Rich People Think About Money (Psychology of Money).*
    https://www.youtube.com/watch?v=rdctz6zSMKw
14. YouTube. *How Rich People Think About Money (Psychology of Money).*
    https://www.youtube.com/watch?v=rdctz6zSMKw
15. Clason, George S., and Horowitz, Mitch. *The Richest Man in Babylon (Original Classic Edition).* Gildan Media. 2019.

16. Dictionary. *Assignment.*
    https://www.dictionary.com/browse/assignment
17. American Dictionary of the English Language
    (1828). *Dominion.*
    https://webstersdictionary1828.com/Dictionary/domi
    nion
18. YouTube. *How and Why I Do Business Like King
    Solomon.*
    https://www.youtube.com/watch?v=BFQshdoHT7o
19. American Dictionary of the English Language
    (1828). *Sin.*
    https://webstersdictionary1828.com/Dictionary/sin
20. American Dictionary of the English Language
    (1828). *Debt.*
    https://webstersdictionary1828.com/Dictionary/debt
21. American Dictionary of the English Language
    (1828). *Debtor.*
    https://www.thefreedictionary.com/debtor
22. Dictionary. *Testament.*
    https://www.dictionary.com/browse/testament
23. Anderson, William C. *A Dictionary of Law.* T. H.
    Flood and Company Law Publishers. Chicago, IL.
    1889.
24. American Dictionary of the English Language
    (1828). *Testament.*
    https://webstersdictionary1828.com/Dictionary/testa
    ment
25. American Dictionary of the English Language
    (1828). *Testament.*

https://webstersdictionary1828.com/Dictionary/testament

26. American Dictionary of the English Language (1828). *Covenant.* https://webstersdictionary1828.com/Dictionary/covenant

27. Life Hope and Truth. *Joint Heirs With Christ.* https://lifehopeandtruth.com/prophecy/kingdom-of-god/joint-heirs-with-christ/

About the Author

(2024)

Pao Chang is the author of RevelationKnowledge.net. In 2021, he gave his life to Jesus, the Christ, and became a born-again man of God. Pao loves to study the Holy Bible, God's Law, and the power of words. He also loves to travel with his wife and share the wisdom of God with believers and non-believers.